*Clearly this adoration of the cacao bean in all of its manifestations has not left the French consciousness,*

*Nor is it likely ever to do so*

Suzanne C Toczyski
Professor of French

*Above Image: Courtesy of Lampe Berger, "Hymne au Chocolat"*

*Ladurée, a Parisian favorite for chocolate and macaroons*

*A fabulous creation at the Salon du Chocolat in Luxembourg*

"Chocolate French" concept created and edited by André K. Crump

Cover Design: André K. Crump, Heather McDonald of McDonald Design

Additional writing contributions from: Bernard Poussin, Dr. Suzanne C. Toczyski, Paule Caillat, Gerri Chanel, Daphne L. Derven, Julie Baker, Joan Osburn, P Segal, Robert Steinberg, Isabelle Alexandre, Dorothée Mitrani-Bell, Diana Barrand, Cara Black, Clay Gordon

Photo Credits: TCB-Cafe Publishing, Debauve & Gallais, Jean-Paul Hévin, Zoe Bistro, Karin Smith, Joan Osburn, New Orleans Tourism Marketing Corp., Chocoland/The Chocolate Show/Salon du Chocolat, Expogast, French Pastry School, Cafe Matou, Foires Internationales de Luxembourg, Teuwen One Image, Left Bank, La Note, John Lehmann, Mars chocolate, Le Fleuriste du Chocolat, Le Cordon Bleu, Bouchon, Broussards, and many other great chocolatiers and restaurateurs.

Many thanks are due to all the restaurants, bistros, schools, organizations, chefs and individuals who provided us with these great recipes, as well as to Gilles Kubler, Robyn Cahill, Le Cordon Bleu, L'Académie Française du Chocolat et de la Confiserie, l'Alliance Française, Lycée Français la Perouse, Sur la Table, Caffe d'Amore, Christina Valhouli, COPIA, Dan Hayes, GraceAnn Walden, Jim Kastleman, PaperCity Magazine, John Mariani, Paul Comi, Rocky Randall, Ronald Margulis, Susie Shoaf, Deborah Kwan Public Relations, Foires Internationales de Luxembourg, Anne Reuter, Lisa Kajita, Brussels Fairs & Exhibitions, Marianne Nelissen, Madame Figaro magazine, New Orleans Convention & Visitor Bureau, Kathleen Iudice, Joie de Vivre Hospitality, Alan Parowski, Pink Frankenstein, Holly Krassner, Teuwen One Image, Layla Almazooqi, Catalina Bajenaru, Stephanie Green Crump, Chandler Crump, Anise Crump, Georgia Peterson de Machuca, Laura Claverie, Stephanie Teuwen, Eleanor Bertino Public Relations, Guittard Chocolate, Newtree Chocolate, Scharffen Berger Chocolate Maker, Vosges Haut-Chocolat, Lake Champlain Chocolates, Fran's Chocolates, Victoria Voicehowsky, CHOCOA, Soho Press, Gerard Pitchford, Matt Blair, Laura Smith Blair and the staff at the Canvas Cafe & Gallery, Tony Baldini, and Mel @ Cafe Claude

## tcb cafe publishing

PO Box 471706
San Francisco, CA 94147

First Edition Copyright © 2004, TCB-Cafe Publishing
Second Edition Copyright © 2006, TCB-Cafe Publishing
Third Edition Copyright © 2011, TCB-Cafe Publishing
Cover Copyright © 2004, tcb cafe publishing

ISBN 0-9822200-7-3
Printed in the United States of America

# CHOCOLATE FRENCH

## 3RD EDITION

# CONTENTS

# RECIPE INDEX

Ce qui n'est pas clair n'est pas français.

*That which isn't clear is not French.*

**- Rivarol**
**French writer**

Ne croyez pas que le chocolat soit un substitut à l'amour... L'amour est un substitut au chocolat.

*Don't believe that chocolate is a substitute for love... Love is a substitute for chocolate.*

**- Miranda Ingram**

Le bon chocolat ne vous rendra pas malade. Il ne vous fera même pas grossir.

*Good chocolate won't make you sick. It won't even make you gain weight.*

**- Robert Linxie**
**French chocolatier**

Les personnes qui boivent régulièrement du chocolat se distinguent par leur bonne santé et leur résistance à toutes sortes de maladies mineures qui troublent la sérénité de la vie.

*People who regularly drink chocolate are distinguished by their good health and their resistance to all sorts of minor illnesses that disturb the serenity of life.*

**- Anthelme Brillat-Savarin**
**Gastronome et magistrat français**

Prenez du chocolat afin que les plus méchantes compagnies vous paraissent bonnes.

*Take chocolate, so that the most unpleasant company seems good to you.*

**- Marquise de Sévigné**
**French woman of letters and Parisian aristocrat**
**to her daughter in January 1672**

# FOREWORD

Why do we French so love our chocolate?

Chocolate came to France in the middle of the 17th century through Spain. It was a terrible tasting brew, a mix of cocoa and sugar, but also of many different spices whose final aroma had nothing in common with the flavours of today's chocolate. In fact, chocolate-making was not yet sophisticated enough that the product offered to demanding Royale palates could be served without several masking flavours. Ironically Spain, because of the winds of fashion, saw their love for chocolate begin to wane at the time. The French court and aristocracy, on the other hand, generated an absolute frenzy for pure chocolate, an obsession which spread among large portions of the population through the 18th and 19th centuries.

In this environment *obsedé*, generations of French artisans have worked diligently to perfect their craft. This chocolate, without strong spices and adding only cane sugar - quite specific to French tastes for true 'chocolate noir' with a minimum of 50% of cocoa - has survived through the ages. It has succeeded in making this journey without losing its soul, still made by crafstmen, in a world dominated by an industrial pattern of marketing chocolate 'as poor in cocoa as it is rich in sugar.'

The French are therefore quite proud of their chocolate, and those inspired by their traditions and culture.

Bernard Poussin, CEO
Ste Debauve & Gallais
Maison fondée en 1800
Fournisseur des anciens Rois de France
30, rue des St Pères 75007 Paris

# INTRODUCTION

*Français au chocolat*. It means, "Chocolate French," which is the title of this book. I thought it was appropriate because so many chocolate dishes in French are described as "au chocolat." *Poires au chocolat* (pears and chocolate), *gateau au chocolat* (chocolate cake), *tarte au chocolat* (chocolate tart). If these concoctions were mediocre in execution, no one would really care what they were called. But they aren't. Invariably they are excellent, memorable, and perhaps, transcendental.

Chocolate is a magical element. In medieval times there was believed to exist a Sorcerer's Stone, an implement which could transmogrify lead into gold, or age into youth. Chocolate has those properties. By taking this one ingredient, and various proportions of water, sugar, butter or cream, a chef can literally produce hundreds of different creations. Ganache, fondants, pots, mousse, even sorbets; so much coming from so little. Like the legendary Sorcerer's Stone, chocolate can change the most mundane substance into gold, and if not, at least into gold-flecked truffles.

Chocolate today is a global phenomena, as likely to cause a stir at a child's birthday party or a Valentine's Day dinner as it was to incite passion and competition at the Royal Court in Versailles.

If you've ever been to France, you know that it is difficult to walk down the street without coming across some type of chocolate-infused object. *Pain au chocolat, croissants au chocolat, éclairs, rochers, palets d'or, gaufres, crêpes, madeleines*... the list goes on and on. In store windows, on cafe menus, in bistros and brasseries, chocolate is almost as common in France as an actual French citizen. Of course, this experience is not limited to France. You can encounter similar situations in French-speaking countries like Belgium and Switzerland. These Francophonic countries have thoroughly embraced their chocolate-loving French heritage. Belgium is a major exporter of cocoa goods, and Switzerland is home to some of the largest chocolate companies in the world. The French influence on chocolate doesn't stop in Europe. Across the globe, in cities such as New York, San Francisco, Chicago, Sydney, Montreal, Tokyo, Los Angeles and New Orleans, you can see and taste the impact of "Chocolate French" in recipes of all types.

Chocolate for me holds many dear memories. When I was a university student in Dijon, I once rode a train from London to the English Channel, took the midnight ferry across, caught another train to Paris, then switched to a third train for Strasbourg. During this marathon journey, the only items in my luggage aside from clothes were: a) three bottles of water, b) two *baguettes*, and c) five bars of chocolate. By the time I reached Strasbourg, I was on my last chocolate bar with a crust of bread, and I still felt fantastic. There were several things that I could have complained about during the trip, but the food wasn't one of them.

Of course, on the train wasn't the only place where chocolate played a large role in my life. Across the street from my school in Dijon was a small *patisserie/chocolatier*. In the store window were always rows and rows of sweets and candies. Those confections were indeed quite entrancing, but what held my interest were the *éclairs*. As éclairs go they were not very large, yet they had fresh chocolate icing on top and were filled with delicious, mouth-watering cream. Usually the patisserie only made about ten each morning, so if I didn't arrive early enough then they would all be gone. At least three days a week I found myself rushing to school, not so much as to be on time for class (like that would actually happen), but to get at least one of these heavenly pastries. After that experience, I find it difficult to disagree with the possibility that the height of luxury might not be an expensive car, a yacht in Monte Carlo, or a villa in Jamaica, but may instead be a really, really, really good chocolate éclair.

One of my favorite French expressions is, "*ça va de soi.*" It means in essence, 'that goes without saying,' or 'that's obvious.' When we decided to create a cookbook on the subject of French and chocolate, essentially a 'chocolate lover's guide to French,' we had two reactions from those who heard the

concept. The first was, 'Wow, that sounds great!" The second was, "*Ça va de soi.*"

Apparently the connection was obvious.

*Andre K Crump*
Publisher

# A BRIEF HISTORY
## THE LOVE AFFAIR BETWEEN FRANCE & CHOCOLATE

While chocolate is perhaps associated more readily by many with Switzerland (Lindt and Nestle) and, perhaps to a lesser extent, Belgium (Godiva, Côte d'or), it has a remarkably rich history in France dating from the early seventeenth century. Introduced to Europeans subsequent to Christopher Columbus's excursions in the Caribbean, it is the explorer Cortés who is most often credited with presenting the honorable substance, in beverage form, to the court of Spain in 1510. At that time, however, chocolatl (a mixture of ground cacao and maize sweetened with honey and flavored with tlilxochitl) was in extremely short supply, and even Philip II of Spain had to ration it. The first non-alcoholic stimulant drink to arrive in Western Europe, beating both coffee and tea by over a century, chocolate's history is somewhat obscure due to the destruction of many historical records, but its fascination for the French in particular has been well-documented from the outset, beginning in the seventeenth century.

*Chocolate was officially registered as a medical substance in the French Pharmaceutical Codex*

From the time of its official introduction in France by Anne of Austria upon the occasion of her marriage to Louis XIII, and perhaps even before, since Catholic friars traveling through Europe helped to make the beverage known throughout the continent, chocolate's wondrous and sometimes frightening powers were touted in medical documents, correspondence, dictionaries, and even paintings. Early literature cites chocolate's ability to aid digestion, intoxicate, and arouse. Its curative qualities were credited with the ability to adjust the humors of the body and heal a plethora of ills, including fever, inflammation, stomach upset, spasms, coughing, and constipation. Many believed chocolate also had the power to cause hallucinations, which is perhaps not surprising, as the substance was occasionally mixed with Psilocybe mexicana (a possible psychedelic known as "little brown mushrooms"). Often praised as an aphrodisiac, chocolate was said to inflame passions and enhance sexual potency and female sensuality. A wide variety of ingredients from anise to almonds, cinnamon to chiles, even musk, ambergris, rose petals and orange water, were added to the substance to enhance its stellar qualities (or, a skeptic might say, to disguise inferior beans that had traveled long and far to arrive on the European continent). Sold in apothecaries beginning in 1758, when it was officially registered as a medical substance in the French Pharmaceutical Codex (a collection of approved drug formulas), cacao was believed by some to be a panacea for all human ills, while more suspicious souls denounced it as an instrument of necromancers and sorcerers, a perilous vice leading to certain damnation. While fears regarding chocolate's potential spiritual consequences waned fairly quickly, belief in its medical properties remained prevalent even into the early twentieth century—and some of us remain convinced of its therapeutic qualities to this day.

During the sixteenth and early seventeenth centuries, cacao dominated as Spain's most important crop, and its trade and consumption in Europe remained the monopoly of that country. French interest in chocolate as a beverage spiked thanks to royal infatuation with the substance. Anne of Austria's maids are said to have circulated the most successful recipes throughout the French court, and her successor, Marie-Thérèse, wife of Louis XIV, went so far as to appoint a royal chocolate maker. Indeed, she and her brother, the Duc d'Orléans, apparently consumed copious amounts of chocolate, though her husband did not share or even claim to understand his wife's obsession with the intoxicating beverage. Though Spain had been keeping the prized beverage a secret for over a century, that country lost its monopoly on cacao partly as a result of this royal marriage. The French began cultivating cacao in Martinique and Saint-Lucia in the mid-seventeenth century, and the expansion of sugar cane plantations in that same region contributed to the boom of chocolate consumption. Marie-Thérèse also introduced the first chocolatières in France, elaborate chocolate pots and chocolate services made of gold, silver, pewter or porcelain, with openings for special swizzle sticks at the top used to whip the liquid into a frothy delectation. High import taxes kept the price of chocolate relatively high throughout the seventeenth century, and in 1670 Paris still had only one chocolate merchant. Seventeenth and eighteenth-century printmakers such as Bonnart included domestic scenes of ladies and gentlemen enjoying a cup of chocolate in their work, and the beverage became a hot topic of conversation in the salons at the time. The Church did not consider the consumption of chocolate to break the fast (though it was judged more nourishing than mutton and beef), and wealthy ladies went so far as to have the drink served during long sermons at Mass.

Writing to her daughter Madame de Grignan in 1671, the famous literary épistolière Marie de Rabutin-Chantal, the Marquise de Sévigné chronicles her own personal, rather complicated history with the substance, at times touting its benefits, at others complaining of its ill effects. Learning that her daughter has not been sleeping well, Sévigné claims that "Le chocolat vous remettra," but expresses concern because Mme de Grignan has not yet acquired the chocolatière necessary to prepare the beverage properly in her far-away residence in Provence. Like many of her contemporaries, Sévigné focuses primarily on chocolate's purportedly medicinal qualities in her letters. Only two months after this strong endorsement of chocolate's restorative qualities, however, Sévigné has completely reversed her judgment of the substance, and she blames her susceptibility to the "latest fashion" as responsible for her temporary infatuation:

Le chocolat n'est plus avec moi comme il était; la mode
m'a entraînée, comme elle fait toujours. Tous ceux qui m'en
disaient du bien m'en disent du mal. On le maudit; on
l'accuse de tous les maux qu'on a. Il est la source des
vapeurs et de palpitations; il vous flatte pour un temps, et
puis vous allume tout d'un coup une fièvre continue, qui
vous conduit à la mort. Enfin, mon enfant, le Grand Maître,
qui en vivait, est son ennemi déclaré; vous pouvez penser
si je suis d'un autre sentiment. Au nom de Dieu, ne vous
engagez point à le soutenir; songez que ce n'est plus la mode
du bel air. [15 April 1671]

She even goes so far as to suggest, later that year, that she is profoundly
angered by chocolate (she claims to be "fâchée contre lui personnelle-
ment"), blaming it for a particularly bad bout of colic that has tormented
her, and four months later, she remains "brouillée avec le chocolat." She
is especially suspicious of the substance and its potentially nefarious
effects on her daughter's pregnancy, and cites a recent case in which a
marquise of her acquaintance drank so much chocolate during her own
pregnancy that her child, when born, was "noir comme le diable" and
died shortly thereafter. Fortunately, Sévigné dares to try chocolate again
on the advice of Mme de Grignan, her daughter (who has spoken, in
a letter to her mother, of "l'étonnement de [ses] entrailles" caused by
her own chocolate consumption); Sévigné is ultimately pleased with
the results: "J'ai voulu me raccommoder avec le chocolat; j'en pris
avant-hier pour digérer mon diner, afin de bien souper, et j'en pris hier
pour me nourrir, et pour jeûner jusqu'au soir. Il me fit tous les effets
que je voulais; voilà de quoi je le trouve plaisant, c'est qu'il agit selon
l'intention." In sum, she fell back in love with it again.

*In the seventeenth and eighteenth
century the beverage became a hot
topic of conversation in the salons at
the time*

Chocolate is also the subject of this extensive entry in the 1690 Dictionnaire universel  of Antoine Furetière.

CHOCOLATE. s.m. Confection ou meslange de drogues dont
on fait un breuvage, & même un remede, qui nous est venu
des Espagnols, qui l'ont apporté des Mexicains, chez lesquels
ce mot de chocolate signifie simplement confection. D'autres
disent que c'est un mot Indien composé de latté, qui signifie
de l'eau, et de choco, mot qui est fait pour exprimer le bruit
avec lequel on le prepare, comme témoigne Thomas Gage.
Sa base ou principale drogue est le cacao, fruit d'un arbre
du même nom. Anthoine Colmenero de Ledesma Chirurgien
Espagnol en a fait un Traitté, & voicy la composition qu'il en
fait, qui est la plus usité.

Sur un cent de cacao on mesle deux graines de
chile ou poivre de Mexique, ou en sa place du poivre des
Indes, une poignée d'anis, de ces fleurs qu'on appelle petites
oreilles, ou dans le pays vinacaxtlides, & deux autres qu'on
nomme mecachusie, ou au lieu de celles-cy, la poudre de
six roses d'Alexandrie, appellées roses pâles, une gousse
de campesche, deux drachmes de canelle, une douzaine
d'amandes & autant de noisettes d'Inde, & la quantité
d'achiotte qu'il faudra pour luy donner couleur. Toutes ces
plantes sont descrites par de Laët. On broye le tout, on en
fait une paste ou conserve avec de l'eau de fleur d'orange,
qui le durcit fort; & quand on en veut prendre, on le delaye
dans de l'eau bouillante avec un moulinet.

Il n'en faut pas boire durant les jours Caniculaires,
ni de celuy qui est frais fait depuis un mois. Le Pere
Escobar dit qu'étant pris en liqueur, il ne rompt point le
jeusne, quoy que ce soit un mets tres-nourrissant. Le Cardi-
nal François Marie Brancaccio en a fait un Traittee particulier
pour soustenir la mieme opinion, quoy que Stabbe Medecin
Anglois ait fait un autre Traitté qui montre qu'on tire plus
d'humeur nourrisante d'une once de cacao, que d'une livre
de bœuf, ou de mouton. Il est si commun en la nouvelle
Espagne, qu'il consume par an plus de 12.millions de livres
de sucre. Les Espagnols estiment que la derniere misere où
un homme puisse être reduit, c'est de manquer de chocolate,
car c'est leur boisson ordinaire. Ils ne la quittent que quand
ils peuvent avoir quelque autre boisson qui enyvre. On dit
qu'il aide à la digestion, qu'il rafraischit les estomacs trop
chauds, & qu'il eschauffe ceux qui sont trop froids. Mr. Du
Four a aussi fait un Traitté du Chocolate, du Thé & du Caffé.
Barthelemy Maradon Medecin Espagnol a condamné l'usage
du chocolate. Chaque livre de chocolate vaut à Mexique 52 s.

This remarkable entry, which includes not only multiple etymologies of the word, but also its history, usage, related recipes and spices, medical pertinence, cost and economic impact, and a bibliography of related treatises on the subject, gives a sense of the progress chocolate made in the minds (and mouths) of its consumers over the course of only eighty years.

By 1705, a royal edict permitted café owners to sell chocolate by the cup, as they were already doing with coffee, which had itself been introduced in France only in 1615. In fact, coffee was one of the primary bases used to prepare chocolate as a beverage; cacao was also mixed with water, wine, and beer, although it was not mixed with milk until 1727 in England. Chocolate became the fashionable beverage of the boudoir, and to be admitted to the "Regent's chocolate" was considered a special honor. The first chocolate factory in France was located in Bayonne, where a guild of chocolatiers had existed since 1761. That city exported chocolate to various European cities. Sailors were happy to find chocolate included in their rations, and chocolate was similarly popular as a drink in the French colony of Québec, where it was sold in taverns and cafés. Thomas Jefferson, a familiar face in Parisian circles, hoped

*Chocolate became the fashionable beverage of the boudoir and to be admitted to the Regents chocolate was considered a special honor*

chocolate would eventually replace tea and coffee as a more salubrious stimulant. In 1778, the first hydraulic machine for crushing and mixing chocolate paste appeared in France, an invention which greatly simplified production of the high-demand substance.

Artists, writers and intellectuals were similarly smitten with chocolate as a beverage. In 1760, a painter named Jean-Etienne Liotard found himself at the court of Austria with a commission to paint a portrait of the empress Maria Theresa and her family. During that period, he also painted a picture of a young woman, possibly the chambermaid who served him breakfast every morning, carrying a pot of his favorite breakfast drink. (Some speculate the painting is, in fact, a portrait of the empress herself.) This painting, called La Belle Chocolatière, has long since graced containers of American-manufactured Baker's chocolate. Libertines, too, jumped into the chocolate frenzy. In the works of the Marquis de Sade, chocolate is reputed to restore the depleted sexual fluids of the over-sexed libertine, and is touted as an important dietary supplement throughout Sade's œuvre, becoming a kind of fetish object for that reason. One of his characters even kills his own mother with a poisoned cup of the beverage, proving once again the dangerous capacities of the seductive substance.

Sade himself was reputed to be a passionate gourmet who fancied baked apples, vanilla custards, quail stuffed with grape leaves, very fresh cream of chard soups and, of course, chocolate cakes. One of Sade's acquaintances, Louis Petit de Bachaumont, chronicles an evening chez Sade during which the incorrigible libertine, who enjoyed "experiment-ing" with various medical substances, was said to have served pastilles laced with powdered Spanish fly, provoking an orgy of mythic propor-tions. In 1772, Sade, traveling with his valet Latour, organized a soirée with four young ladies whom he regaled with little chocolate candies. Bachaumont writes: "I am told that the Count de Sade, who in 1768 caused great disorder by his crimes with a woman on whom he wanted to test a new cure, has just played in Marseilles a spectacle at first amusing but later horrible in its consequences. He gave a ball to which he invited many people and for dessert gave them very pretty chocolate pastilles. They were mixed with powdered 'Spanish flies.' Their action is well known. All who ate them were seized by shameless ardor and lust and started the wildest excesses of love. The festival became an ancient Roman orgy. The most modest of women could not restrain themselves... [M]any persons died as a result of the excesses and many others still suffer recurrent pains." Court records of the time indicate that Sade actually ended up poisoning four ladies of the evening that night; the suffering young ladies brought charges against the libertine, causing him to be sentenced to death, upon which Sade fled for his life. Later, when he was returned to prison, Sade wrote to his wife, "I wish for a chocolate cake so dense that it is black, like the devil's ass is blackened by smoke." The good woman was most obligining and regularly brought the Marquis chocolate to sweeten his stay in such a miserable place.

*In the works of the Marquis de Sade chocolate is reputed to restore the depleted sexual fluids of the over sexed libertine*

The price of chocolate did not drop significantly until the nineteenth century, when the drink truly became available to the masses as the powdered form of the substance was retailed in France. Bayonne's 1822 trade calendar quotes more than twenty prestigious chocolate firms in France at that time. In the early nineteenth century, the famous Menier family chocolate business established itself, first in the Marais neighborhood of Paris, and later in Noisiel, on the banks of the Marne. Jean-Antoine-Brutus Menier is credited with inventing chocolate-coated medicine as well a revolutionary new design concept for "household chocolate," which was sold in individually wrapped bars. (Several Swiss chocolatiers, including Lindt, Suchard and Nestle, established their businesses during this same period.)  Again, literary and cultural figures do not neglect this powerful substance in their writings. Brillat-Savarin's 1826 Physiologie du Goût continues to promote chocolate as good for the health (particularly for those suffering from advanced stages of pylorus) and pleasant to consume – de rigueur as an accompaniment to the morning meal to keep oneself in shape. Balzac, on the other hand, credited the discovery of chocolate by the Spanish as the source of their failed plans for world empire: "Who knows whether the abuse of chocolate has not had something to do with the debasement of the Spanish nation, which, at the time of the discovery of chocolate, was about to recreate the Roman Empire."

Twentieth-century French authors and artists have continued to muse on the power and possibilities of chocolate. Tristan Tzara's complete works include the following lines of verse: "Mangez du chocolat  / lavez votre cerveau / dada / dada / buvez de l'eau," but chocolate was not entirely a positive image for the poet, which he associated primarily with the sickeningly sweet values of moral society. Marcel Duchamp's Broyeuse de Chocolat (Chocolate Grinder), a component of a larger composition, Le Grand Verre (The Large Glass), is not only a Dada piece par excellence but also a serious celebration of eroticism inspired by an actual chocolate grinder the artist saw in the streets of Rouen and the artist's own association of chocolate with seminal fluid. Duchamp was particularly

fascinated by the potential mingling of the senses elicited by the incorporation of chocolate – either in image form, or as an actual artistic medium – into his artwork. (His painting Moonlight on the Bay of Basswood from 1953 was done in ink, pencil, crayon, talcum powder and chocolate.) Many pages of Duchamp's work notes are devoted to the mixing of different colors to evoke all possible shades of chocolate, and he believed that the viewer should spend up to an hour absorbing all of the various levels of sensation created by his paintings.

A French nursery rhyme suggests that the French love of chocolate begins in infancy: *Fais dodo / 'Colas mon petit frère; / Fais dodo / T'auras du lolo / Maman est en haut, / Qui fait du gateau; / Papa est en bas, / Qui fait du chocolat.* Clearly, this adoration of the cacao bean in all of its manifestations has not left the French consciousness, nor is it likely ever to do so.

*Suzanne C Toczyski*
*Professor of French*

Fais dodo,

Colas mon petit frere

Fais dodo,

tu auras de l'eau, l'eau

Maman est en haut

Qui fait du gateau

Papa est en bas

Qui fait du chocolat

*I remember the first time I visited France, aged around 10, and discovered that here was a nation where you could have a cup of hot chocolate accompanied by a pain au chocolat for breakfast. And no-one seemed to think that particularly indulgent. Coming from a culture of tea and toast I found that very impressive indeed. I think this was my first inkling that the French might be enjoying a superior quality of life.*

**- Dan Hayes, Editor**
**CNN Traveller magazine, London**

*Ever since I first discovered that croissant could be measurably improved by the addition of a slab of chocolate, I've been a cheerful devotee of pain au chocolat- -the ultimate bread and chocolate. Makes me wish I were a French schoolchild coming home for a cup of cafe au lait and pain au chocolat instead of Graham Crackers and milk, although those have their great appeal to me too. Way better than a madeleine and sip of lime tea!*

**- John Mariani**
**Esquire Magazine Food Editor**

*Chocolate heaven for me is three things - all French kissed. A bite-sized truffle from XOX Truffles in San Francisco; a small molten chocolate cake first-created by chef John George Vongreichten (JoJo, Vong and others) and lastly, but not the least, a finger full of my late French Canadian mother's chocolate cookie recipe, straight from the mixing bowl.*

**- GraceAnn Walden**
**San Francisco Bay Area Restaurant Columnist**

*Right: Selections from Lake Champlain Chocolates, in Vermont*

This Page: The innovative selections at Roy Chocolatier, 27 rue de Longchamp, Paris

Opposite Page: The luxurious orange and lemon flavors of Mademoiselle de Margaux Chocolates

# MELTING CHOCOLATE

Almost all recipes in this book that use chocolate instead of cocoa powder require the chocolate to be melted. When we say, "Melt the chocolate," refer to one of the following techniques:

**Melt the chocolate**

*Technique #1:*

Put the coarsely chopped chocolate in a heat-proof bowl. Set bowl on top of a bain-marie or saucepan that has water nearly simmering over low heat. Be sure that the water does not touch the bottom of the bowl, nor does any water get into the chocolate. Stir the chocolate occasionally based on type (dark, milk, white) with a plastic spatula or wooden spoon.

*Technique #2: Microwave*

Put the coarsely chopped chocolate in a microwave-proof bowl. Place in microwave on Medium setting. Heat for 1 1/2 to 2 minutes. When in microwave, melting chocolate may not appear to melt or change shape. After 1 1/2 minutes check to see if chocolate is softening or has acquired a shiny surface texture. If so, stir and set aside, or stir and place back in microwave for the remainder of time. Note that "Medium" may be #5 or #6 on a scale of 1 to 10, etc., depending on your microwave oven.

*How often to stir when melting chocolate:*

- Stir dark chocolate occasionally

- Stir milk chocolate frequently

- Stir white chocolate continuously

## Melting Chocolate with Cream, Butter, or Milk

*"Melt the chocolate and butter" or "Melt the chocolate and milk"*

Chopped chocolate can be melted in a saucepan over low heat along with cream, milk or butter, or can be added to the already heated cream and butter to melt.  Stir frequently until chocolate is melted and incorporated.

## Tempering Chocolate

1. To temper chocolate couverture, melt chopped chocolate in a bowl. Stir the chocolate occasionally based on type (dark, milk, white) with a plastic spatula or wooden spoon.

2. Remove from heat.

3. When chocolate has cooled, reheat for about 1-2 minutes.

*Photograph courtesy of Mars*

# CHOCOLATE GANACHE

A nearly ubiquitous element of French chocolate cuisine, ganache can be used as a filler for truffles and other sweets, or as a glaze or filling for cakes. Essentially a mixture of chocolate and cream or milk, the result is a fascinating example of the ever malleable properties of cacao.

1. IN SAUCEPAN, BRING CREAM TO A LOW BOIL. REMOVE FROM HEAT.
2. PLACE CHOPPED CHOCOLATE IN A BOWL. ADD HOT CREAM. STIR SLOWLY TO ALLOW CHOCOLATE TO MELT AND INGREDIENTS TO COMBINE.
3. CONTINUE TO STIR FOR 1-2 MINUTES.

**10 OZ. DARK CHOCOLATE, CHOPPED (USE CHOCOLATE WITH A HIGH PERCENTAGE OF CACAO, SUCH AS COUVER-TURE QUALITY)**

**1 CUP HEAVY CREAM**

# CHOCOLATE GANACHE

### French Pastry School, Chicago

1. CHOP THE CHOCOLATE INTO PIECES. MAKE SURE CHOCOLATE IS AT ROOM TEMPERATURE. PLACE PIECES IN A BOWL.
2. BRING THE MILK AND CREAM TO A BOIL IN A SAUCEPAN.
3. POUR THE MILK AND CREAM OVER THE CHOPPED CHOCOLATE, AND LET THE MIXTURE STAND UNTIL THE CHOCOLATE GANACHE HAS COOLED SLIGHTLY.
4. INCORPORATE ALL THE INGREDIENTS OF THE GANACHE WITH A WHISK FROM THE CENTER OUT.
5. WHEN THE GANACHE HAS COOLED A BIT MORE, MIX A SMALL AMOUNT OF GANACHE WITH THE BUTTER, THEN FOLD THE BUTTER WITH THE REST OF THE GANACHE.

**1/2 CUP DARK CHOCOLATE (70% CACAO)**

**4 1/2 TBS WHOLE MILK**

**3/4 TBS CREAM AT 35%**

**1/4 CUP PLUGRA BUTTER (82%)**

# PRALINE

Praline is a finely chopped, creamy paste of caramelized hazelnuts. It is used in a wide range of chocolate items, such as truffles, ice cream, cakes, tarts, and Madeleines. If you cook French-style chocolate recipes often, it might be convenient to occasionally make a batch of praline to have on-hand.

1. ADD SUGAR, WATER, AND HAZELNUTS TO A SAUCEPAN, AND BRING TO A BOIL. STIR FREQUENTLY UNTIL BOILING, THEN DO NOT STIR.
2. LET CONTINUE TO BOIL UNTIL SYRUP IS A MEDIUM GOLDEN CARAMEL COLOR AND THE HAZELNUTS BEGIN TO POP.
3. POUR PRALINE ONTO A PARCHMENT LINED BAKING SHEET AND ALLOW TO COOL. DO NOT UNDER ANY CIRCUMSTANCE TOUCH OR TASTE THE CARAMEL UNTIL COMPLETELY COOLED - MIXTURE IS EXTREMELY HOT ON BARE SKIN.
4. WHEN COOLED, BREAK PRALINE INTO SMALL PIECES USING A BLENDER, FOOD PROCESSOR, OR ROLLING PIN.

**1 CUP SUGAR**

**1 CUP HAZELNUTS**

**6 TBS WATER**

# CHOCOLATE SAUCE

This sauce is excellent over crêpes, gaufres, and sautéed or poached fruit.

1. SLOWLY BRING BUTTER, SUGAR AND CREAM TO A LOW BOIL IN A SAUCEPAN, STIRRING SO THAT SUGAR DISSOLVES.
2. ADD CHOCOLATE AND REMOVE FROM HEAT. STIR UNTIL CHOCOLATE HAS MELTED AND SAUCE IS A SMOOTH TEXTURE.

NOTE: IF MAKING CHOCOLATE SAUCE AHEAD OF TIME, KEEP WARM IN A BAIN-MARIE OR A BOWL OVER WARM WATER.

**8 OZ. DARK CHOCOLATE, CHOPPED**

**1/2 CUP OF HEAVY CREAM**

**4 TBS UNSALTED BUTTER, CUT INTO SMALL PIECES**

**4 TBS SUGAR**

# CHOCOLATE TARTLET WITH COFFEE CREAM

**Bistrot Bruno Loubet, London,** This is definitely a dessert for chocolate lovers! When perfectly cooked, the soft chocolate filling in the crisp tartlet shell is a wicked surprise!

### SHORTBREAD DOUGH

1. SIFT THE FLOUR ONTO THE WORK SURFACE IN A PILE AND MAKE A WELL IN THE CENTER.
2. PUT THE BUTTER, SALT AND SUGAR INTO THE WELL AND MIX TOGETHER WITH YOUR FINGERTIPS. GRADUALLY WORK IN THE FLOUR. USE THE HEEL OF YOUR HAND TO SPREAD OUT THE MIXTURE AND THEN CRUMBLE IT BETWEEN YOUR HANDS.
3. WHEN THE INGREDIENTS ARE THOROUGHLY COMBINED, MIX IN THE EGG TO BIND INTO A DOUGH.
4. SHAPE INTO A BALL, WRAP AND CHILL FOR AT LEAST 2 HOURS.
5. TO COOK, PREHEAT THE OVEN TO 350ºF
6. ROLL OUT THE DOUGH TO ABOUT 3MM (1/8 INCH THICK) AND CUT OUT 4 DISCS, EACH 10-11 CM (4 TO 4 1/2 INCHES) IN DIAMETER. LINE FOUR 8 CM (3 1/3 INCH) TARTLET MOLDS WITH THE DISCS. PRESS FOIL SMOOTHLY ON TOP OF DOUGH IN MOLDS AND FILL WITH BAKING BEANS OR RICE. BAKE FOR 10 MINUTES OR UNTIL THE PASTRY IS JUST SET.
7. CAREFULLY REMOVE THE FOIL AND BEANS (OR RICE), THEN BAKE FOR A FURTHER 2 MINUTES. SET THE TARTLET CASES ASIDE TO COOL.

### FILLING

1. MELT THE CHOCOLATE, AND SET ASIDE.
2. PUT THE EGGS IN A LARGE BOWL AND ADD 2 1/2 TBS OF GRANULATED SUGAR. SET THE BOWL OVER A PAN OF SIMMERING WATER AND WHISK ENERGETICALLY UNTIL THE MIXTURE IS VERY THICK AND PALE AND IT WILL MAKE A RIBBON TRAIL ON ITSELF WHEN THE WHISK IS LIFTED OUT.
3. ADD THE MELTED CHOCOLATE, MELTED BUTTER AND COCOA POWDER, WHISKING WELL, THEN FINISH WITH THE CORNFLOUR AND ORANGE ZEST.
4. FILL THE TARTLET CASES WITH THE CHOCOLATE MIXTURE. BAKE IN THE PREHEATED OVEN AT 350ºF FOR 6-8 MINUTES OR UNTIL THE FILLING IS SLIGHTLY RISEN.

### FILLING

3 1/2 OZ. OF BITTER CHOCOLATE

2 EGGS

2 1/2 TBS OF GRANULATED SUGAR

2 TBS OF UNSALTED BUTTER MELTED AND COOLED

1/2 TSP OF UNSWEETENED COCOA POWDER

1/2 TSP OF CORN FLOUR

GRATED ZEST OF 1/3 OF AN ORANGE

ICING (POWDERED) SUGAR TO FINISH

### FOR THE SHORTBREAD

USE A READY-MADE SHORTBREAD DOUGH OR USE THE FOLLOWING INGREDIENTS.

1 1/4 CUP OF PLAIN FLOUR

7 TBS OF SOFT UNSALTED BUTTER

A PINCH OF SALT

10 TBS OF ICING (POWDERED) SUGAR, SIFTED

1 EGG

### FOR THE COFFEE CREAM

1 TBS OF INSTANT COFFEE MIXED WITH 3 TBS OF HOT WATER

3/4 CUP OF CRÈME ANGLAISE (OR READY-MADE FRESH CUSTARD)

## Coffee Cream

Meanwhile mix the coffee with the crème anglaise.

## To Serve

1. Spoon the coffee cream onto plates and tilt and rotate to spread the cream evenly.

2. Set a tartlet in the middle of each plate and dust the top with powdered sugar.
   Serves 4.

# Warm Chocolate Puddings with Pistachio Cream and Pears

## Moelleux au Chocolat à la Crème Pistache et aux Poires

**Le Cordon Bleu, Paris,** These little chocolate puddings, served with a sweet pistachio cream and poached pears, are an ideal winter dessert.

### Make the pistachio cream

1. Put the pistachios on a baking sheet or in a pan and toast under a broiler for 1 to 2 minutes, shaking to make sure they do not burn. Remove from broiler and grind the nuts to a paste using a mortar and pestle or a food processor.
2. Pour the milk into a saucepan and heat slowly until just at boiling point.
3. Put the egg yolks and sugar into small bowl and whisk until pale and creamy. Whisk continuously and pour the hot milk into the creamed egg yolks.
4. Transfer the mixture into a clean saucepan and cook gently over low heat, stirring constantly until the mixture begins to thicken and coats the back of a wooden spoon. Remove from the heat immediately. Do not allow the mixture to boil otherwise it will break and become lumpy. Strain into a bowl.
5. Add the vanilla extract, to taste. Whisk in the pistachio paste and chill.

### Moelleux au Chocolat

1. Brush eight 3 x 1 1/2, 1/2-cup soufflé dishes or ramekins with melted butter.
2. Put the chocolate into the top of a double boiler over hot water, off the heat, and allow it to melt slowly. Stir occasionally.
3. Put the softened butter into a bowl and beat until soft and creamy. Stir in the sifted cocoa. Fold the mixture into the melted chocolate.
4. Put the egg yolks in a bowl and add 1/2 cup of the sugar. Beat until doubled in volume, then fold into the chocolate mixture.

### Pistachio Cream

3 Tbs chopped pistachio nuts

1 cup milk

3 egg yolks

3 Tbs sugar

1 to 2 drops vanilla extract

### Moelleux au Chocolat

6 oz. semisweet chocolate, chopped

1/3 cup unsalted butter, softened

1/4 cup unsweetened cocoa, sifted

6 eggs separated

1 cup sugar

Poached or canned pears, drained and sliced, to serve

5. Beat the egg whites until stiff peaks form. Add the remaining sugar and beat to a stiff, shiny meringue. Fold carefully into the chocolate mixture, in three additions, until lightly combined.

6. Spoon into the prepared soufflé dishes in equal quantities. Bake for 25 minutes or until set.

7. Remove from the dishes and place on individual plates. Spoon a little chilled pistachio cream around each. Decorate with sliced pears.

Serve immediately. Serves 8

# CHOCOLATE CROISSANT PUDDING WITH TOFFEE SAUCE, STRAWBERRIES & PECANS

**Cafe de la Presse, Chef Patrick Albert, San Francisco,** Cafe de la Presse is at the epicenter of San Francisco's French Quarter. With over 80,000 French expats living in the San Francisco Bay Area, that's quite a responsibility. Owner Jean Gabriel has his own philosophy on chocolate and French: "Friandise des Marquises, Entremets des Gourmets, Faut bien qu'on se le dise, Rien ne vaut le chocolat Francais!"

## CROISSANT PUDDING

1. ADD VANILLA EXTRACT TO MILK AND WARM MILK UNTIL HOT (BUT NOT BOILING).
2. STIR EGGS AND SUGAR TOGETHER IN A BOWL. ADD MIXTURE TO HOT MILK.
3. SLICE THE CROISSANTS INTO APPROXIMATELY 1-INCH CUBES, THEN ADD THEM TO THE MILK BATTER TO SOAK FOR 3-5 HOURS (PREFERABLY OVERNIGHT).
4. PREHEAT OVEN TO 300ºF.
5. FILL INDIVIDUAL CIRCULAR RING MOLDS WITH BREAD PUDDING MIXTURE. PLACE IN OVEN FOR ABOUT 18 MINUTES, UNTIL SOMEWHAT FIRM.

## TOFFEE SAUCE

1. MAKE A CARAMEL BY ADDING THE SUGAR AND A BIT OF COLD WATER. STIR UNTIL SUGAR IS DISSOLVED, THEN SLOWLY RAISE TEMPERATURE UNTIL WATER IS BOILING (BETWEEN 290º-350ºF). LOWER HEAT UNTIL SYRUP TAKES ON A DARKER COLOR.
2. ADD LEMON JUICE, BUTTER, AND STIR UNTIL BUTTER IS MELTED. ADD CREAM, STIRRING CONSTANTLY.

## CHOCOLATE SAUCE

PLACE MILK, BUTTER, AND CHOCOLATE IN SAUCEPAN AND HEAT OVER LOW FLAME, UNTIL CHOCOLATE IS MELTED. STIR FROM TIME TO TIME UNTIL MIXTURE HAS A SMOOTH, SAUCE-LIKE FINISH.

## TO SERVE

SERVE THE CROISSANT PUDDING WARM WITH CHOCOLATE SAUCE ON TOP AND TOFFEE SAUCE DRIZZLED AROUND PLATE. GARNISH PLATE WITH ALMONDS AND STRAWBERRIES. SERVES 6

## CROISSANT PUDDING

6 CROISSANTS
2 CUPS MILK
6 EGGS, WHOLE
2 OZ. SUGAR
2 OZ. DARK CHOCOLATE CHIPS
1 TBS VANILLA EXTRACT
1 OZ. PECANS, TOASTED
1 PINT STRAWBERRIES, SLICED

## TOFFEE SAUCE

1 CUP SUGAR
1/4 CUP WATER
1/4 CUP BUTTER, SALTED
1/3 CUP HEAVY CREAM
JUICE FROM HALF A LEMON

## CHOCOLATE SAUCE

4 OZ. DARK CHOCOLATE
1/3 CUP MILK
1/2 OZ. BUTTER, UNSALTED

## SPECIAL EQUIPMENT

6 TO 8 RING MOLDS

# CHOCOLATE FONDANT WITH ORANGE CONFIT AND RASPBERRY SAUCE

**The Left Bank, Larkspur, California,** The English translation of "fondant" is "melting." In regard to this recipe, it means 'flowing, melted chocolate.' The Left Bank presents delicious meals that leave you craving more, and when you want to describe this object of desire, try to pronounce it in French: 'fawn-dawnt.'

## CANDIED ORANGE ZEST

1. PLACE THE ORANGE ZEST IN WATER, SIMMER FOR 5 MINUTES AND STRAIN.

2. PLACE THE WATER AND SUGAR INTO A SMALL POT, BRING TO A SIMMER.

3. ADD THE ORANGE ZEST AND SIMMER FOR ABOUT 10 MINUTES OR UNTIL THE ORANGE ZEST IS CRYSTALLIZED. REMOVE AND PLACE ON NAPKIN.

## CHOCOLATE FONDANT

**5 OZ. CHOCOLATE (VALRHONA SEMISWEET)**

**13 TBS BUTTER, UNSALTED**

**7 TBS FLOUR, ALL-PURPOSE**

**4 EGG YOLKS**

**4 EGGS, WHOLE**

**10 TBS SUGAR**

## FONDANT

1. PRE-HEAT THE OVEN TO 400°F.

2. MELT THE CHOCOLATE AND BUTTER.

3. BEAT THE EGGS, YOLKS AND SUGAR UNTIL MIXED THOROUGHLY.

4. ADD THE CHOCOLATE INTO THE EGG AND SUGAR MIX.

5. SIFT THE FLOUR INTO THE CHOCOLATE MIXTURE AND STIR WELL.

6. SPRAY 4 OZ. FOIL CUPS WITH NON-STICK AND DUST WITH COCOA POWDER, THEN FILL 3/4THS OF THE WAY TO THE TOP.

7. PLACE IN OVEN AND BAKE FOR ABOUT FIVE MINUTES.

8. THE CHOCOLATE SHOULD NOT SET IN THE CAKE'S MIDDLE SO THAT WHEN CUT INTO IT OOZES OUT.

## CANDIED ORANGE ZEST

**3 ORANGES (ZEST, ORANGE PART ONLY).**

**1 CUP WATER**

**2 OZ. SUGAR**

## RASPBERRY SAUCE

**1 PINT FRESH OR FROZEN RASPBERRIES**

## RASPBERRY SAUCE

PUREE AND STRAIN RASPBERRIES.

## OTHER

**1 SCOOP COFFEE ICE CREAM**

**MINT GARNISH**

**3 TBS POWDERED SUGAR**

## TO SERVE

1. PLACE THE COOKED FONDANT INTO THE OVEN AT 350°F FOR APPROXIMATELY FIVE MINUTES, UNTIL WARM BUT NOT COOKED.

2. SQUIRT A SMALL AMOUNT OF RASPBERRY SAUCE IN THE MIDDLE OF THE PLATE.

3. UNMOLD THE WARM FONDANT AND PLACE ON THE RASPBERRY SAUCE; SPRINKLE THE ORANGE ZEST AROUND THE PERIMETER.

4. TAKE ONE SCOOP OF COFFEE ICE CREAM AND PLACE TO THE SIDE OF THE FONDANT, THEN SPRINKLE POWDERED SUGAR ON THE PLATE. GARNISH WITH MINT.

### Chocolate, Sensation and Quality

Chocolate wasn't discovered by the French, but we have certainly appreciated it since it was introduced by Anne of Austria, daughter of the King of Spain. Anne married Louis the 13th, and introduced chocolate to the French Court in Paris. Since that time, French artisans keep perfecting the making of chocolate.

The French savant and gourmand Brillat-Savarin once said, "Chocolate is Health." We now know that chocolate is a source of magnesium and an anti-depressant, but we also know also that it is an aphrodisiac as well. For my part, chocolate is like "having an orgasm." You let your taste buds discover some sensation at a different level; the flavor, the richness, the intensity are to the point that your body is in a trance, having goose bumps and shivers.

I am a chocoholic. I eat chocolate every day, but not just any kind. I have to have a burst of sensation in my mouth to completely enjoy those little moment of happiness. Chocolate lovers know that a good chocolate melts on the tongue like butter, has a true aroma of chocolate, and is not greasy or sticky.

French people tend to be more passionate about dark chocolate than we are for milk or white chocolate. This difference in taste and expectation may perhaps explain why the Swiss and Belge are quite good in these other versions of chocolate. The quality of European chocolate is now at its best. With the techniques and the master chocolatiers, it is very competitive. But EU Common Market regulations allowing the use of vegetable fat is a danger to the quality of European chocolate. Thank God, it is prohibited in France, and for the sake of us chocolate lovers let's hope it stays that way

*Chef Isabelle Alexandre*

### About Chef Isabelle Alexandre

Isabelle Alexandre was the chef de cuisine at the Santa Barbara location of Michel Richard's Citronelle. Hand-picked by the legendary Michel Richard, executive chef of the Citronelle restaurants, Ms. Alexandre has a long history of chef positions. These include Epicure in Paris, the historic Old Angler's Inn in Maryland, Le Meridien Park-Atlantic in Lisbon, Pastis Restaurant and Bistro M in San Francisco, and Citronelle in Washington, D.C. A native of Toulouse, France, Chef Alexandre studied at the Vatel Cooking School in Paris, L'Ecole Hotelière de Lausanne in Switzerland, and trained at George Blanc in Vonnas, France, a Michelin three-star restaurant renowned for its nouvelle cuisine.

# Marquise au chocolat

**Chef Isabelle Alexandre, Santa Barbara,** "My first experience eating chocolate was when I was twelve years old. My dad brought us to a bistro, where I discovered a dessert called 'La Marquise au chocolat.' I was in heaven. I wanted to know the recipe and the first thing I did when I got back home was to make that dish. Even now it is a tradition. When I go back home to France I always make that dessert."

1. Melt chocolate with butter. One way is to add the chocolate and butter together in a bowl, then put it on top of a bain-marie or saucepan with nearly simmering water over low heat until the chocolate and the butter are completely melted. Stir occasionally, with a plastic spatula or wooden spoon. Be sure that the water does not touch the bottom of the bowl, nor does any water get into the chocolate.

2. Remove chocolate mixture from the heat and let it cool to room temperature.

3. Add 4 egg yolks into the chocolate batter, incorporate well.

4. Beat all of the egg whites, add a pinch of salt at the beginning of the beating and then when the whites start to get almost firm add 1/4 cup of sugar. A few seconds later add 1/4 cup more of sugar until the egg whites are nice and stiff. Take a large tablespoonful of the beaten egg whites and slowly fold it into the chocolate batter using a spatula. Add little by little the rest of the beaten egg whites until well incorporated.

5. Transfer chocolate batter into a terrine mold or loaf pan and place in the freezer for about 2 to 4 hours, until the chocolate Marquise is nice and hard.

6. Remove from the freezer and then demold it by turning the mold upside down and put it under hot water till it starts to slide down.

17 oz. bitter sweet chocolate (58% cocoa)

8 oz. or 14 Tbs of unsalted butter (recommend Plugra, European style)

8 eggs (whites separated from yolks)

1/2 cup of granulated sugar (1/4 cup and 1/4 cup - 2 steps)

A pinch of salt

To Serve

Marquise may be sliced and served with a creme anglaise (vanilla sauce).

# CHOCOLATE MOUSSE CHARLOTTE

## CHARLOTTE AU CHOCOLAT

**La Note Restaurant Provençal, Dorothée Mitrani-Bell, Berkeley, California,**
"The reason I do what I do is because I believe that the ceremonial aspect of eating is being lost. It is as if most of us never fully commit to the experience of eating. Few people take the time every day to prepare soulful food in a personal environment and share it with family and friends. I love to inspire people to focus on eating as a very deep human moment. To eat is to feel the colors around us, to hear and understand others, and to respect the world we inhabit."

### MOUSSE

1. MELT THE CHOCOLATE (PER INSTRUCTIONS ON PAGE 28).
2. PUT EGG WHITES IN BOWL, ADD PINCH OF SALT, AND WHIP UNTIL WHITES FORM FIRM PEAKS.
3. FOLD MELTED CHOCOLATE INTO EGG WHITES UNTIL MIXTURE IS COMPLETELY CHOCOLATÉ. REFRIGERATE UNTIL READY TO USE.

### FILLING & BODY

1. COOK RASPBERRIES WITH BROWN SUGAR FOR 8-10 MINUTES OVER MEDIUM HEAT, THEN REMOVE FROM HEAT AND ALLOW TO COOL.
2. ADD RUM TO WARM WATER. QUICKLY DUNK EACH LADY-FINGER COOKIE INTO LIQUID, THEN SET THE LADY-FINGER INTO AN OPEN SPACE IN THE CHARLOTTE MOLD, FLAT-SIDE FACING THE MOLD. COVER THE ENTIRE BOTTOM AND SIDES OF THE MOLD WITH MOISTENED LADY-FINGERS.
3. POUR HALF OF THE CHOCOLATE MOUSSE ON THE BOTTOM OF THE MOLD, SPREADING ACROSS TO THE EDGES AS MUCH AS POSSIBLE.
4. PLACE THE RASPBERRIES OVER THE CHOCOLATE.
5. COVER WITH A LAYER OF RUM-MOISTENED LADY FINGERS.
6. ADD A LAYER OF CRÈME FRAÎCHE TO THE SIDES.
7. ADD THE REMAINDER OF THE CHOCOLATE MOUSSE TO THE TOP LAYER AND COVER WITH ANOTHER LAYER OF RUM-MOISTENED LADY FINGERS, FLAT SURFACE SIDE FACING DOWN. THIS WILL BE THE BASE. MAKE SURE THE LADY FINGERS COVER ENOUGH AREA SO THEY WILL SUPPORT THE CHARLOTTE. PRESS DOWN INTO PLACE USING SMALL PLATE.
8. CHILL FOR 4 HOURS.

### TO SERVE

1. REMOVE THE SMALL PLATE.
2. TAKE A LONG, SMOOTH-EDGED KNIFE AND CAREFULLY GO AROUND THE EDGES OF THE MOLD, PUSHING

### CHOCOLATE MOUSSE

**10 EGG WHITES**

**8 OZ. (1/2 LB.) OF MELTED SEMISWEET CHOCOLATE, SUCH AS GUITTARD**

### FILLING & BODY

**3 TBS BROWN SUGAR**

**1/2 CUP OF CRÈME FRAÎCHE**

**3 TBS RUM**

**1 PINT OF FRESH RASPBERRIES**

**1-2 PACKAGES OF LADY FINGERS (APPROXIMATELY 50 PASTRIES)**

**2 CUPS WARM WATER**

**SPECIAL EQUIPMENT**

**MOULE À CHARLOTTE - CHARLOTTE MOLD, FOUND AT COOKING STORES, 6/12 DIAMETER X 4 1/2 HEIGHT**

AGAINST IT BUT BEING CAREFUL NOT TO SCRAPE THE LADY-FINGERS OFF OF THE
CHARLOTTE.

3. TAKE A LARGE SERVING PLATE AND PLACE OVER MOLD (WHERE SMALL PLATE WAS) AND TURN
MOLD OVER, ALLOWING THE CHARLOTTE TO SLIP FROM THE MOLD AND ONTO THE PLATE.

4. PRESENT WITH EITHER CRÈME PATISSERIE, A FRUIT COULIS, OR AS IS.

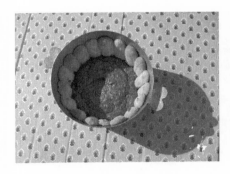

*Step 2 - beginning*

*Step 2 - end*

*Step 3*

*Step 4*

*Step 7*

### Charlotte au chocolat: Filling and body assembly

The chocolate world produces hot new talent each season, and some say
that these three are among the hottest.

Above: Maribel Lieberman of MarieBelle
Below: Katrina Markoff, Vosges Haut Chocolat
Opposite Page: Chocolatier Fritz Knipschildt

# Young Turks of
# Great chocolate

## CHOCOLATE BARDOT

Chocolate continually inspires all types of cultural creativity in France, even in non-culinary fields. French film star Brigitte Bardot has also inspired a large amount of French creativity. With roles in movies such as Godard's *Le Mépris* (Contempt) and *Masculin - Féminin*, And *God Created Woman*, *Helen of Troy*, and *Viva Maria!*, Bardot is known worldwide as the prototypical French "sex symbol." Time magazine declared her one of the 20th century's Twenty Most Beautiful Stars, calling her "the princess of pout, the countess of come hither... that brought a whole new audience to French films." Needless to say, Brigitte Bardot has incited passions that almost equal those aroused by chocolate, no small feat in France.

### Brigitte Bardot
**Dario Moreno (autres interprètes: Star Academy 2001)**

*[excerpt]*
"Brigitte Bardot Bardot
Brigitte béjo béjo
Je crois bien que je t'aime
Autant que le chocolat "

*[translation]*
Brigitte Bardot Bardot
Brigitte béjo béjo
I really think that I love you
As much as chocolate

# CHOCOLATE RED WINE SOUP WITH STRAWBERRIES

This recipe was originally inspired by one presented by legendary chef Michel Richard in his book, "Home Cooking with a French Accent."

1. IN A LARGE BOWL, MIX TOGETHER THE WINE, VANILLA AND SUGAR. STIR WELL TO MAKE SURE THAT THE SUGAR IS DISSOLVED.

2. ADD SLICED STRAWBERRIES TO WINE AND MARINADE AT ROOM TEMPERATURE FOR 3 HOURS.

3. MELT CHOCOLATE.

4. STRAIN THE WINE MARINADE, AND PLACE STRAINED STRAWBERRIES IN SEPARATE BOWL.

5. HEAT STRAINED WINE MARINADE OVER LOW FLAME UNTIL IT REACHES THE SAME TEMPERATURE AS THE MELTED CHOCOLATE.

6. WHISK 3-4 TABLESPOONS OF THE WINE MARINADE INTO THE MELTED CHOCOLATE, MAKING SURE THAT THE COMBINED MIXTURE IS OF A SMOOTH TEXTURE. SLOWLY STIR IN THE REMAINING WINE MARINADE. WHISK TO FULLY INCORPORATE TOGETHER INTO A SOUP.

7. REMOVE FROM HEAT AND STRAIN THE SOUP THROUGH A FINE SIEVE INTO A LARGE BOWL.

8. ALLOW SOUP TO COOL TO ROOM TEMPERATURE, THEN ADD RESERVED STRAWBERRY SLICES FROM STEP 4.

9. PLACE SOUP IN REFRIGERATOR TO CHILL FOR APPROXIMATELY 5 HOURS.

## TO SERVE

SPOON INTO SOUP BOWLS AND GARNISH WITH A LARGE STRAWBERRY. SERVES 2-4

1/2 CUP GRANULATED SUGAR

1 CUP ZINFANDEL, CABERNET SAUVIGNON, OR PINOT NOIR

1 PINT STRAWBERRIES, DE-STEMMED AND THINLY SLICED LENGTHWISE

3 OZ. BITTERSWEET DARK CHOCOLATE, FINELY CHOPPED

1 TBS VANILLA EXTRACT

6 LARGE STRAWBERRIES, WITHOUT STEM, AS A GARNISH

Le chocolat. J'ouvre toujours avec beaucoup de precaution une tablette de chocolat. Je ne déchire pas l'emballage et j'en fais une véritable cérémonie.

*Chocolate. I love chocolate so much that I always open it very cautiously, being careful not to tear the wrapper. I turn it into a real ceremony.*

**- Olivier Picasso**
**grandson of Pablo Picasso**
**on the topic of Symbols of Hedonism**

Je ne connais rien de plus érotique qu'une tablette au fort pourcentage de cacao.

*I know of nothing more erotic than a bar of chocolate with a high percentage of cocoa.*

**- Paul-Loup Sulitzer**
**French writer and finacier**

Heureux chocolat, qui après avoir couru le monde, à travers le sourire des femmes, trouve la mort dans un baiser savoureux et fondant de leur bouche.

*Happy chocolate, who after having crossed the world, across the smiles of women, finds death in the delicious melting kiss of their mouths.*

**- Anthelme Brillat-Savarin**
**Gastronome et magistrat français**

*My most memorable chocolate experience involved getting covered in it -- there was plenty of French chocolate and French kissing too. I was paid to "review" three types of chocolate body paint so I roped in my boyfriend to give it a go.*

**- Christina Valhouli**
**Travel Writer**
**Forbes**

*Right: The countertops of chocolate selections at La Maison du Chocolat in Paris*

## Chocolate Salons

In France there are three kinds of non-political gatherings whose very natures compel the average French citizen to attend. The first is a jazz concert. Though an American-born art form, jazz has found a loving and charitable godmother in France. Jazz instrumentalists that are barely known in North America have huge and dedicated followers on the Hexagon. So loyal are they that at one point it became absolutely surreal, and if you had not seen or heard from your favorite jazzman in the States for the last five years, you would try looking in France.

The second type of gathering that excites the French are auto shows. For a country where it takes a lot of study and money for the average person to become licensed and own a car, it amazes foreigners that the "fraternité" part of "Liberté, Égalité and Fraternité" might also apply to French automobiles. The French love their cars, but not in a Californian, "I need to have my car or I don't exist" kind of way. Rather, the French see in autos a balance of art, engineering, and style. Car shows, therefore, as the temples of cars, have an extremely reverent group of attendees.

The third type of gathering that energizes the French are *Salons du Chocolat* (Chocolate Shows). If jazz lovers are surreal and auto aficionados are cult-like, then those who take part in the Salons du Chocolat have reached a level which could only be described as metaphysical -- and they are legion.

The largest and most prestigious Salon in France is the Salon du Chocolat in Paris, with over 100,000 attendees and normally taking place at the Louvre. Here, over 150 exhibitors participate in *dégustations* (tastings), presentations, classes, and various competitions. Organizations such as the *Université du Chocolat* direct more than 50 sessions, while in other halls topics are addressed like, "Nutella seen by a Master Chef." Awards are also presented to the Best of Show, including Best Truffle and Best Ganache-filled Creation. There are even events for children, much in keeping with the French tradition of early indoctrination into *français au chocolat*.

Explaining how this Salon was started, event founders and producers Sylvie Douce & François Jeantet say, "We met around a passion for chocolate - at a chocolate tasting.  Together, we created the Salon du Chocolat in Paris, followed by the Chocolate Show in New York, Tokyo, and Luxembourg."

What is a Salon du Chocolat like? It depends on your objective. If you want to meet new contacts and new chefs, it's like a fantastic country club. If you want to learn new techniques and recipes, it's like

*A sweet festival for everyone*

*Salon du Chocolat founders Sylvie Douce & François Jeantet*

an enormous accelerated classroom. If you want to taste all kinds of chocolate from islands, countries, and artisans from around the world, it's like... paradise. The most important equipment to take with you are a pen, some bread, and a large bottle of water.

The Salon du Chocolat obviously originated as a French concept. Points out Paris Salon du Chocolat founders Sylvie Douce & François Jeantet, "The French 'tongue' has such a taste for chocolate because chocolate is linked to our childhood. Traditionally, French children have a *tartine au chocolat* (bread, butter and a piece of dark chocolate) when they get back from school. France also has by tradition a passion for food and cuisine. Chocolate is a product of the *terroir* (the specific land, soil conditions and climate of a region that creates a specific taste in the resulting chocolate, wine or coffee harvest), and French people are very interested in the notion of terroir, which is the basis of wine production here. Consumers found in chocolate a new way to learn about varietals, terroir, and taste."

Outside of Paris are numerous Salons du Chocolat as well. Each varies depending on the year, region, and organizing group. One such event is the "*Magie du Chocolat*" ("Magic of Chocolate") salon produced by the Corporation des Patissiers, Confiseurs, Chocolatiers et Glaciers du Bas-Rhin. This group has attracted up to 15,000 visitors to their show in the city of Strasbourg.

Of course, it would be quite limiting to only look for Salons du Chocolat in France. Belgium is an excellent spot for a tantalizing chocolate show. One such show is the industry event known as CHOCOA. This international chocolate trade show takes place in Brussels, with the goal of giving Belgian chocolate and its ambassadors their own forum. Chocolate producers, manufacturers, and specialists from over 40 countries attend, network, make deals, and "*dégustent*." Belgian 'grand nom' Barry Callebaut also uses this forum to present the International Belgian Chocolate Award, the winner of which is given the title, "Ambassador of Belgian Chocolate" for two years.

New York, Luxembourg and Tokyo are also the locations of respected Salons that are associated with the Salon du Chocolat in Paris. The New York Chocolate Show is quite large, and attracts attendees from all of North America, as well as from Europe, South America and Asia. The Luxembourg Salon du Chocolat takes place in connection with the Expogast (i.e. Expo and Gastronomy) & Culinary World Cup events, a relationship which assures an ample and sophisticated turnout of over 40,000 visitors. The Culinary World Cup is a major attraction, as it places a number of different establishments in direct competition, including national teams from Sweden and Switzerland, hot young chefs, patissiers, chocolatiers, confiseurs, and grand masters. In combination with the Salon du Chocolat, these two huge events are worth the trip to this petite and charming country.

## CHOCOLATE FASHION

Voila! As with so many things French, even at gastronomic events the twin elements of fashion and style are not far removed. Such is the case at the Salons du Chocolat ("Chocolate Shows"). Because of the high tensile strength of tempered chocolate, and its ability to be molded into almost any shape, chocolate has long been a material of haute couture.

Many a designer has taken up the challenge of creating the most glamorous outfit they can imagine, "tout en chocolat." There is nothing quite like watching a line of beautiful women, a chain of handsome men, and a score of stunning hats and gowns in chocolate slink up and down the catwalk.

Both participants and spectators find these Salon du Chocolat fashion shows ("*défilés*") quite thrilling. Not only is there energy and innovation, but there is also the possibility that some new talent will yet be discovered. A few of the well known designers who have taken part in the Paris, New York, Tokyo and Luxembourg fashion shows   include Sonia Rykiel, Chantal Thomass, Paco Rabanne, Olivier Lapidus, and Fernando Guzman.

For the uninitiated chocolate lovers who attend the show, there may be another reason for their excitement.  They may mistakenly believe that the clothing could melt, leaving a totally naked model on the stage, dripping in ganache. We hate to disappoint them, but though the lights may be hot, the chocolate is very, very cool.

*"Choquanet" by Martin Howard, pastry chef at Brasserie & Brasserie 8 1/2, NYC*

**Made in Chocolate:**

*Valrhona dress by Kim O'Flaherty, pastry chef for Valrhona*

*Carmen Marc Valvo, designer with Yvan Lemoine, pastry chef at Fleur de Sel, NYC*

Aimez le chocolat à fond, sans complexe ni fausse honte, car rappelez-vous: "sans un grain de folie, il n'est point d'homme raisonnable."

**- La Rochefoucauld
Moraliste et homme politique français**

Le chocolat est, plutot que le nectar ou l'ambroisie, la vraie nourriture des dieux.

*Chocolat is, rather than nectar or ambrosia, the real food of the gods.*

**- Joseph Bachot**

Mon désir de chocolat a rarement diminué, même en période de grand péril.

*My desire for chocolate has rarely diminished, even in times of great peril.*

**- Marcel Desaulnier, Master Chef**

La vie est comme le chocolat, c'est l'amer qui fait apprécier le sucre.

*Life is like chocolate, it's the bitter that makes you appreciate the sweet.*

**- Xavier Brebion**

## CHOCOLATE BEAUTY

How many ways can a body use chocolate without actually eating it? This is not a question in France, where chocolate, or at least an inference of chocolate, has long been used as a vital component of makeup and hair care products. Not a season goes by in which at least three major fashion or lifestyle magazines publish a makeup or clothing story based on a chocolate-theme, nor does a quarter pass in which at least three talk about the health benefits of chocolate.

One women's magazine, for example, entitled a feature article, "The Virtues of Chocolate." The article began with the premise that, "Le chocolat n'est pas une mechante tentation, mais au contraire un aliment plaisir qui regorge de micro-nutriments (Chocolate is not a sinful temptation, quite the contrary, it is a pleasure food packed with micronutrients). A doctor from a well-known French health spa then goes on to explain how cacao has relaxing and stimulating virtues. "Chocolate secretes a veritable magic cocktail of amphetamines, magnesium and caffeine, which promotes at the same time both calm and energy. The magnesium regulates the nervous system, and acts as both a sedative and a relaxant."

In an issue of another women's magazine, editors outlined how brunettes could enhance their looks by using various chocolate-themed makeup products. A few of their recommendations included:

> "For those with chestnut hair, - 'Le chocolat glace de Camille Albane.' This frosted brown suits all those who detest red highlights (Marron Toffee, Camille Albane)."

> "'Le bois d'acajou (mahogany wood) de Patrick Ales.' This technique makes chestnut hair vibrate. First the colorist puts on the base color, then to imitate the grain of the wood they use different color tones: miel (honey), caramel, cafe (coffee), chocolat. The effect resembles varnished mahogany. (Terre de Feu, Patrick Ales)."

> "Cremes gourmandes." Skin also hungers for sweetness, so we spread over it savory milks and appetizing exhalations. "Lotion pour le Corps au sucre, Baume Hydratant au chocolat..., chez Fresh, la beauté n'est qu'un dessert ." (Hydrating Balm au chocolat, beauty is only a dessert.)

Yet another magazine included fashion spread based on a chocolate-theme, as well as more recommendations for makeup, hair and skin care.

**beauté**

## Recettes de beauté...
# CHOCOLATÉES !
• Coulée cacao dans les cheveux pour réveiller les
• châtains et chocolat chaud sur la bouche ou la paupière.
• Une nuance à croquer !

**CHEVEUX : recettes au cacao**
Les coloristes font leur « cuisine » en coulisse. Le résultat ? Des reflets chauds dans les cheveux.
● **CHRISTOPHE ROBIN :** « Avec le chocolat, je choisis toujours une tonalité plus claire que celle des yeux et des produits qui contiennent très peu d'oxydant pour éviter que le marron ne vire au rouge avec le temps. Si vous avez quelques taches de rousseur et des yeux noisette, n'hésitez plus, le chocolat, c'est pour vous ! Au choix : les couleurs unies et ton sur ton qui donnent de la densité aux cheveux qui manquent de pep. Ou bien les balayages qui animent les cheveux de reflets sans changer la couleur de base. » Tél. : 01.42.60.99.15.
● **RODOLPHE :** « Je l'aime en touches. J'utilise un cataplasme aux plantes qui colore et gaine les cheveux (Eos de Wella). Ou encore les "transparences antillaises", un balayage décliné sur quatre couleurs : du châtain clair cuivre au blond foncé. À réchauffer avec une coulée de henné ardent. » Tél. : 01.42.61.46.59.
● **RÉGINA chez Massato Colors :** « Un châtain naturel n'est jamais uni, il est fait d'une multitude de reflets, qui vont du doré au marron glacé. Pour retrouver ce dégradé de tonalités, j'ai mis au point l'effilage. Une couleur que nous appliquons sur cheveux secs. Ensuite, pour obtenir un résultat fondu, nous effaçons sur les longueurs en la diluant avec de l'eau. Et, pour obtenir un camaïeu de marrons, nous repigmentons ces longueurs avec des pigments naturels. » Tél. : 01.45.48.87.92.

### Les salons du chocolat
● **CHEZ CLAUDE MAXIME,** la tendance est aux couleurs « fourrure » : vison, renard, castor. Pour casser l'uniformité, une nouvelle technique : les « couleurs cristallines ». Il s'agit d'une poudre de coquille d'huître que l'on mélange au produit de coloration. Résultat : ces microbilles imperméabilisent le cheveu par endroits pour une couleur très nuancée. Tél. : 01.53.23.03.05.
● **CHEZ JEAN-CLAUDE BIGUINE :** le balayage fauviste. Dans un premier temps, on isole les mèches du dessus de la tête. On applique de façon homogène sur le reste de la chevelure un produit de coloration blond cuivré profond. Ensuite, on colore les mèches de recouvrement avec un blond rouge. Résultat : ce teint, « ... » sur une couleur dorée, fait flamboyer la chevelure ! Tél. : 01.53.67.51.00.
● **CHEZ JEAN-MARC MANIATIS :** « Toutes les couleurs chocolatées et les blonds vanillés ont le vent en poupe. En revanche, les reflets rouges sont bannis. » Deux techniques à adopter selon votre longueur de cheveux : le voile de couleur pour les cheveux mi-longs ou longs mais imperativement dégradés ! ou le glaçage pour les cheveux courts. Toutes deux ont le même principe : colorer les mèches de surface dans un ton assez tranché par rapport à la base. » Tél. : 01.47.23.30.14.
● **CHEZ CAMILLE ALBANE :** « C'est exactement fauve ! » nous dit-elle. Dans ce salon réputé pour ses roux, le choix est vaste : bain oriental (soin colorant au henné), métissage de couleur (sans toucher aux racines, on travaille les pointes et les demi-longueurs) et mèches au henné ou balayage vénitien pour une mise en relief plutôt qu'une couleur unie. Le roux se travaille avec subtilité : en coulée sur les pointes pour mettre en valeur un carré lisse ou, pour les cheveux frisés, une coloration qui démarre par du chocolat aux racines pour se terminer en couleur safranée sur les pointes. Cette astuce de coloration donne de la légèreté aux boucles. Tél. : 01.46.33.59.57.
● À noter : vingt-deux coiffeurs de Paris, de la région parisienne et province se sont groupés pour signer la

# Bouchon Chocolate Tart

**Bouchon, Yountville and Beverly Hills, California and Las Vegas, Nevada,**
Bouchon is a sister establishment of Thomas Keller's world famous culinary temple,
The French Laundry. Though a bit more relaxed and décontracté, Bouchon's food is also
world class. Says founding chef Jeff Cerciello, "I think chocolate is the most versatile of
all ingredients. It lends a voluptuous feel to any dish and is perfect in any state: soft,
hard, cool, warm, even frozen. Without it, no meal is complete, no menu as tantalizing.
Truly a gift from the gods!"

## Hazelnut Crust

1. In a coffee or spice grinder, grind the sugar with the hazelnuts and place in a mixing bowl along with the salt.
2. Add the butter and cream the mixture until smooth.
3. Gradually add the flour until the dough comes together and forms a mass. Add a little cold water as necessary for the dough to hold together.
4. Remove the dough from the mixer, place on a flat surface, and form into a disc. Wrap in plastic wrap and let chill in the refrigerator for at least an hour before rolling.
5. Butter and flour a 10 to 10 1/2 inch tart pan with removable bottom.
6. Flour the countertop surface or board and roll the dough into a circle to about 3/8 inches thick. Flour the dough and board as necessary to keep it from sticking. Roll the dough up around the rolling pin and place in the tart pan. Gently lift the edges to allow the dough to fill the corners of the pan, making the dough a little thicker around the edges. Remove excess overhanging dough. Be sure that the wall is about 1/4-inch thick and that there are no thin spots. If there are, pat a little of the leftover dough to create a wall of even thickness.
7. Prick the bottom of the crust with a fork and refrigerate for at least 15 minutes before baking.
8. Preheat oven to 375ºF.

## Hazelnut Crust

- 3 Tbs granulated sugar
- 1/3 cup hazelnuts, blanched, ground
- 1 tsp kosher salt
- 10 Tbs unsalted butter
- 1 3/4 cups all-purpose flour
- Butter and flour for the tart pan

## Chocolate Mousse

- 4 1/2 ounces Valrhona Manjari or other bitter-sweet chocolate, finely chopped
- 2 Tbs sweet cream butter, diced
- 2 Tbs hot water or espresso
- 1 cup heavy cream
- 3 large eggs, separated
- 1 Tbs granulated sugar

- 1/2 cup hazelnuts, toasted, chopped
- Cocoa powder

9. TO BAKE: FILL THE TART WITH A PIECE OF PARCHMENT PAPER OR ALUMINUM FOIL AND FILL WITH DRY BEANS. DO NOT 'PUSH' THE BEANS IN OR THEY MAY DAMAGE THE DOUGH. BAKE FOR ABOUT 20 MINUTES OR UNTIL THE CRUST IS A LIGHT GOLDEN BROWN. DO NOT RUSH THIS PROCESS. IF THE BEANS ARE REMOVED TOO EARLY, THE SIDES OF THE CRUST WILL SHRINK.

10. REMOVE THE BEANS AND PARCHMENT AND RETURN THE CRUST TO THE OVEN TO COOK FOR ANOTHER 15 TO 20 MINUTES OR UNTIL THE DOUGH IS A RICH GOLDEN BROWN.

11. REMOVE THE TART AND LET IT COOL COMPLETELY IN THE PAN PLACED ON A COOLING RACK.

## CHOCOLATE MOUSSE

1. WHIP THE CREAM TO SOFT PEAKS AND REFRIGERATE.

2. MELT THE CHOCOLATE, BUTTER, AND WATER OR ESPRESSO IN A SAUCEPAN OVER LOW HEAT. WHEN THE CHOCOLATE HAS MELTED, REMOVE FROM THE HEAT. CONTINUE STIRRING UNTIL THE CHOCOLATE IS JUST SLIGHTLY WARMER THAN BODY TEMPERATURE. TO TEST, DAB SOME CHOCOLATE ON YOUR BOTTOM LIP. IT SHOULD FEEL WARM. IF IT IS TOO COOL, THE MIXTURE WILL SEIZE (HARDEN) WHEN THE OTHER INGREDIENTS ARE ADDED.

3. IN THE MEANTIME, WHIP THE EGG WHITES. WHEN THEY ARE FOAMY AND BEGINNING TO HOLD SHAPE, SPRINKLE IN THE SUGAR AND BEAT UNTIL SOFT PEAKS FORM.

4. WHEN THE CHOCOLATE HAS REACHED PROPER TEMPERATURE, STIR IN THE YOLKS. GENTLY STIR IN ABOUT 1/3 OF THE REFRIGERATED WHIPPED CREAM. NEXT, FOLD IN 1/2 OF THE EGG WHITE MIXTURE UNTIL INCORPORATED, THEN THE REMAINING WHITES AND FINALLY THE REMAINING CREAM. DO NOT OVERMIX; FOLD THE INGREDIENTS JUST ENOUGH TO BE INCORPORATED.

## TO ASSEMBLE

TO COMPLETE THE TART, PLACE THE FINISHED MOUSSE IN A PASTRY BAG AND PIPE INTO THE TART SHELL. SMOOTH THE SURFACE WITH AN OFFSET SPATULA. REFRIGERATE UNTIL READY TO SERVE.

## TO SERVE

JUST BEFORE PLATING, SPRINKLE THE SURFACE OF THE TART WITH THE CHOPPED HAZELNUTS AND DUST THE TOP WITH A LIGHT SPRINKLING OF COCOA POWDER. NOTE: TRY TO USE HAZELNUTS WITHOUT SKINS. IF THEY ARE NOT AVAILABLE, LIGHTLY TOAST THEM AND RUB IN TOWELS TO REMOVE SOME OF THE SKINS.

*This account of Haendel appeared in the April, 1910 issue*
*of the* Revue de Paris. *It discusses his obsession with*
*creating, and the emotional state in which his servants*
*would find him when they brought his morning cup of*
*chocolate. Note that the cup of chocolate, by the way, was*
*the only acceptable reason for disturbing his isolation.*

### Haendel  (excerpt in French)
### by Romain Rolland, Revue de Paris, 15 avril 1910

Le besoin de créer était si tyrannique qu'il avait fini par l'isoler
du reste du monde. "Il ne se laissait," dit Hawkins, interrompre
par aucune visite futile; et l'impatience d'être délivré des idées
qui affluaient constamment à son cerveau le retenait presque
toujours enfermé. "Sa tête ne cessait de travailler; et, tout à ce
qu'il faisait, il ne s'apercevait plus de ce qui l'entourait. Il avait
l'habitude de se parler si haut que chacun savait ce qu'il pensait.
Et quelle exaltation, quels pleurs, en écrivant! Il sanglotait, en
composant l'air du Christ: He was despised. - "J'ai entendu
raconter, dit Shield, que quand son domestique lui apportait son
chocolat, le matin, il restait souvent surpris à le voir pleurer et
mouiller de ses larmes le papier sur lequel il écrivait. " - A propos
de l'Halleluyah du Messie, il citait lui-même les paroles de saint
Paul : " Si j'étais dans mon corps, ou hors de mon corps, en
l'écrivant, je ne sais pas. Dieu le sait. "

*Kohler and*
*Suchard, two*
*well-known and*
*popular brands*
*of European*
*chocolate from*
*the 1900's.*
*Suchard, a Swiss*
*company,*
*created in 1901*
*the extremely*
*successful milk*
*chocolate bar,*
*Milka.*

# WARM CHOCOLATE CAKE WITH VANILLA

**Restaurant Lulu, San Francisco,** A favorite dessert of Bay Area Francophiles and chocolate lovers for over 10 years. Since 1992 Restaurant Lulu has been one of San Francisco's top dining destinations for French-Provencal cuisine.

1. IN A MIXING BOWL OVER A DOUBLE-BOILER MELT THE BUTTER, EXTRA BITTER CHOCOLATE, COCOA AND VALRHONA CHOCOLATE, STIRRING OCCASIONALLY. DO NOT LET IT GET TOO WARM, JUST ABOVE ROOM TEMPERATURE.

2. COMBINE THE VANILLA EXTRACT, SALT AND EGG YOLK AND MIX INTO THE CHOCOLATE MIXTURE.

3. WHIP THE EGG WHITE AND CREAM OF TARTAR TO STIFF PEAKS, THEN ADD THE SUGAR.

4. GENTLY FOLD ABOUT A QUARTER OF THE WHIPPED WHITES INTO THE CHOCOLATE TO LIGHTEN IT. THEN GENTLY FOLD THE CHOCOLATE INTO THE REMAINING WHITES.

5. GENTLY SPOON THE BATTER INTO BAKING TINS THAT HAVE BEEN BUTTERED AND FLOURED. FILL TO ABOUT TWO-THIRDS FULL. PLACE THE TINS IN THE REFRIGERATOR FOR AT LEAST TWO HOURS, OR AS LONG AS OVERNIGHT.

6. TAKE THE TINS DIRECTLY FROM THE REFRIGERATOR AND PLACE THEM IN A PREHEATED 400 DEGREE OVEN AND BAKE FOR 10 MINUTES. REMOVE FROM THE OVEN AND INVERT THE TINS ONTO THE SERVING PLATES. GENTLY LIFT THE TINS AND THE CAKES SHOULD REMAIN ON THE PLATE. IF A CAKE STICKS TO THE TIN, RUN A SMALL KNIFE AROUND THE EDGE OF THE TIN AND ATTEMPT TO UNMOLD THE CAKE ONCE AGAIN.

7. SERVE IMMEDIATELY WITH YOUR FAVORITE ICE CREAM OR DESSERT SAUCE. SERVES 4-6

1/2 LB. BUTTER

1/2 LB. EXTRA BITTER CHOCOLATE

1/4 CUP COCOA POWDER

1/2 LB. VALRHONA CHOCOLATE

1 TBS VANILLA EXTRACT

1/8 TSP SALT

1 EGG, SEPARATED

3/4 CUP SUGAR

1 TSP CREAM OF TARTAR

## *Chocolat et cerises*
**Paroles et Musique: Gilbert Laffaille**

*[excerpt]*

Le vent chaud de l'été
Souffle sur sa chemise,
Il pense a son goûter,
Chocolat et cerises,

*[translation]*

The warm wind of summer
Blows on his shirt
He thinks about his afternoon snack
Chocolate and cherries

# CHOCOLATE-BING CHERRY CAKE

**Absinthe Brasserie, San Francisco,** Absinthe's chefs always strive to match the quality of their food to the warm conviviality of this popular restaurant. This chocolate-Bing cherry cake is certain to bring a bit of joie de vivre to your table.

### CHOCOLATE CAKE

**3 EGGS**

**1 CUP BUTTERMILK**

**1 CUP SOUR CREAM**

**1 1/2 CUP SUGAR**

**1/2 CUP UNSWEETENED COCOA POWDER**

**1 CUP ALL PURPOSE FLOUR**

**1 TSP BAKING SODA**

**1 TSP BAKING POWDER**

**1/2 CUP DRIED CHERRIES**

**3/4 CUP MELTED BUTTER, UNSALTED**

### BING CHERRY SAUCE

**1 CUP SAUTERNES**

**1/2 CUP WATER**

**1/4 CUP LEMON JUICE**

**2 CINNAMON STICKS**

**3 STAR ANISE**

**48 BING CHERRIES, PITTED**

### WHITE CHOCOLATE SAUCE

**3 OZ. WHITE CHOCOLATE, CHOPPED**

**1 TO 2 TBS WATER**

### CAKE

1. BEAT THE EGGS UNTIL THEY HAVE TRIPLED IN VOLUME.

2. ADD THE BUTTERMILK AND SOUR CREAM AND MIX WELL.

3. SIFT TOGETHER SUGAR, COCOA, FLOUR, BAKING POWDER AND BAKING SODA, ADD TO THE BATTER, AND MIX WELL.

4. STIR IN MELTED BUTTER AND FOLD IN THE DRIED CHERRIES.

5. POUR THE BATTER INTO A BUTTERED, FLOURED, 9x12 INCH PAN.

6. FILL A ROASTING PAN HALFWAY WITH SIMMERING HOT WATER. PUT CAKE PAN INSIDE THE ROASTING PAN (WATER BATH) AND BAKE AT 350ºF FOR APPROXIMATE-LY 1 HOUR AND 15 MINUTES, UNTIL THE CAKE SPRINGS BACK WHEN LIGHTLY PRESSED IN THE CENTER, OR UNTIL AN INSERTED WOODEN SKEWER COMES OUT CLEAN.

7. REMOVE CAKE FROM ROASTING PAN AND OVEN. ALLOW CAKE TO COOL SLIGHTLY, THEN INVERT PAN ON CUTTING BOARD AND RELEASE CAKE FROM PAN.

8. CUT CAKE INTO TRIANGULAR WEDGES.

## Bing Cherry Sauce

1. Bring the sauternes, water, lemon juice, cinnamon, and star anis to a boil.
2. Add the whole cherries and bring back to a boil.
3. Remove the cherries from the liquid and set them aside.
4. Reduce the liquid over medium heat. Remove from heat.
5. Add 12 cherries to the reduced liquid and puree for 2 minutes, then strain.

## White Chocolate Sauce

1. Melt white chocolate.
2. Whisk together melted white chocolate and water to create a sauce consistency.
3. Keep in a warm location.

## To Serve

1. Spoon a ring of white chocolate sauce around the plate.
2. Spoon the Bing cherry sauce in the center of the white chocolate sauce ring, then place the cake slice in the center of the cherry sauce. Place reserved cherries around plate for garnish. Serves 12

# Mexican Chocolate Truffle Torte

**Cafe Andrée, San Francisco,** "As the Mayans once believed that chocolate belonged to the Gods, the French now believe it belongs to them. Leave it to the French to be so audacious; leave it to the French to be so deserving! The Mayans may have worshipped chocolate, but the French made it worthy of worship."

1. Grease & flour cake pans and pre-heat oven to 375ºF degrees.

2. Melt the chocolate and butter together in a saucepan over low heat. Stir occasionally until melted and smooth.

3. In a bowl, beat the sugar into the yolks until pale and fluffy.

4. While the chocolate is still warm, whisk the egg yolk mixture into it, then stir in the flour, almonds and the grated Mexican chocolate.

5. Warm the egg whites slightly and beat until stiff and creamy but not "dry." Fold the whites into the chocolate mixture until just combined.

6. Pour batter immediately into prepared cake pans and bake in the oven for 30 to 40 minutes, or until the cake is completely set around the sides but still a bit "jiggly" in the center.

7. Brush top with Grande Marnier.

**To Serve**

Serve slightly warm with vanilla gelato and sprinkle with additional grated Mexican chocolate.

---

1 1/4 cups butter

7 oz. semi-sweet chocolate, chopped

6 eggs (yolks separated from whites)

1/2 cup brown sugar

3/8 cup sifted flour

3/8 cup finely ground almonds

1 tsp ground cinnamon

A pinch Cream of tartar or cornstarch

1/2 tsp salt

2 oz. grated Mexican chocolate

1 Tbs Grande Marnier

### L'ACADÉMIE FRANÇAISE DU CHOCOLAT ET DE LA CONFISERIE

As many guilds, artisans, and scholars have realized throughout the ages, if you want to be taken seriously then first you must establish a school. In fact, if your art is quite difficult it is even better if you found an Academy. Such is the case with *l'Académie Française du Chocolat et de la Confiserie,* whose goal is to "constitute a morale authority, specific to the craft of chocolate and confections, who is a guardian of tradition and evolution in a framework of professional ethics." Based at 103, rue La Fayette in Paris, this organization was established in 1901, and since that time has diligently pursued its mission to defend and promote French chocolate tradition.

As with the better known l'Académie Française, which confers to define and authorize new French words and phrases, l'Académie Française du Chocolat et de la Confiserie also exercises this responsibility in the realm of chocolate and candy making. One tool they use to accomplish this goal is the publication of a Dictionary of chocolate. The Académie also awards the distinguished *"Prix de l'Académie,"* which is given to persons who through actions, writing, or creation, promote the value of *chocolaterie à la française.*

In addition, as a protector of tradition, l'Académie Française du Chocolat is an avid lobbyist for the use of the logo, 'pure cocoa butter,' a position critical to maintaining the quality of French and Belgian chocolates in the face of expanded competition from other European Union countries.

Of course, with all of this chocolate talent it would be a shame not to share some of it with the public, which is why the Académie publishes a fantastic compilation book of members' recipes. The publication is called, *"Chocolat et Friandises, ou les meilleures recettes de l'Académie Française du Chocolat et de la Confiserie."* A long title indeed, but quite a good book.

L'Académie Française du Chocolat et de la Confiserie is composed of 40 'academics,' plus various 'associates' and 'correspondents,' who together foster the unique culture of *français au chocolat*.

ACADÉMIE FRANÇAISE DU CHOCOLAT ET DE LA CONFISERIE

## *Membres élus à L'Académie Française du Chocolat et de la Confiserie*

| | | | | |
|---|---|---|---|---|
| 1 | Guy | VERDIER | PAU | Confiseur-Chocolatier |
| 2 | Jacques | BELLANGER | LE MANS | M.O.F. Pâtissier-Confiseur |
| 3 | Christophe | CHAMBEAU | PARIS | Confiseur-Chocolatier |
| 4 | Thierry | ATLAN | MONTEVRAIN | M.O.F. Chocolatier-Confiseur |
| 5 | Jean-Paul | HEVIN | PARIS | M.O.F. Pâtissier-Confiseur |
| 6 | Yves | THURIES | CORDES SUR CIEL | M.O.F. Pâtissier-Confiseur-Glacier |
| 7 | Jean-Claude | MENARD | TOURS | Chocolatier |
| 8 | Nikita | HARWICH | ST GERMAIN EN LAYE | Professeur des Universités |
| 9 | Guy | URBAIN | PARIS | Fondateur du Salon INTERSUC |
| 10 | Henry | LE ROUX | QUIBERON | Pâtissier-Chocolatier |
| 11 | Jean-Pierre | RICHARD | ROCHETAILLEE S/SAONE | M.O.F. Chocolatier-Confiseur |
| 12 | Francis | BOUCHER | PARIS | Pâtissier-Chocolatier |
| 13 | Philippe | WASTERLAIN | CHAMONIX | Chocolatier |
| 14 | Christian | CONSTANT | PARIS | Chocolatier |
| 15 | Henri | CHAVERON | PARIS | Docteur d'Etat en Sciences Appliquées |
| 16 | Michel | BELIN | ALBI | Pâtissier-Chocolatier |
| 17 | Jean-François | CASTAGNE | MAZAMET | M.O.F. Chocolatier-Confiseur |
| 18 | Jean | JARRIGES | MOULINS | Chocolatier |
| 19 | Xavier | CONRAUX | BEAUVAIS | Confiseur-Chocolatier |
| 20 | Jacques | DAUMOINX | PARIS | Chocolatier-Confiseur |
| 21 | Gérard | MOYNE-BRESSAND | NIMES | M.O.F. Pâtissier-Chocolatier |
| 22 | Fabrice | GILLOTTE | DIJON | M.O.F. Chocolatier-Confiseur |
| 23 | Alain | URBAIN | PARIS | Commissaire du Salon INTERSUC |
| 24 | Marie-Paule | BERNARDIN | VINCENNES | Ecrivain Gastronomique |
| 25 | Stéphane | BONNAT | VOIRON | Chocolatier-Confiseur |
| 26 | André | BOUCHER | LE HAVRE | M.O.F. Pâtissier-Confiseur |
| 27 | Serge | GRANGER | MONTRICHARD | M.O.F. Pâtissier-Confiseur |
| 28 | Marcel | DERRIEN | PLAISIR | M.O.F. Pâtissier-Confiseur |
| 29 | Annie | PERRIER-ROBERT | VILLAMBLAIN | Ecrivain Gastronomique |
| 30 | Hervé | ROBERT | ENGHIEN LES BAINS | Médecin Nutritionniste |
| 31 | Dominique | MICHEL | VILLECRESNES | Historienne Gastronomique |
| 32 | André | ROSSET | GRENOBLE | M.O.F. Chocolatier-Confiseur |
| 33 | Serge | COUZIGOU | BIDART | Pâtissier-Confiseur |
| 34 | Edouard | HIRSINGER | ARBOIS | M.O.F. Chocolatier-Confiseur |
| 35 | Philippe | BERTRAND | BAILLY | M.O.F. Chocolatier-Confiseur |
| 36 | Daniel | GIRAUD | VALENCE | M.O.F. Pâtissier-Confiseur |
| 37 | Katherine | KHODOROWSKY | PARIS | Metteur en scène gastronomique |
| 38 | Hervé | THIS | BUC | Physico-chimiste |
| 39 | Michel | BAREL | MONTPELLIER | Expert en Cacao |
| 40 | Jean-Paul | BRANLARD | LEVALLOIS | Docteur d'Etat, Maître de conférences Droit Alimentaire |

*A sample membership roster for L'Académie Française du Chocolat et de la Confiserie*

# CHOCOLATE MACAROON À L'ANCIENNE

**Jean-Paul Hévin, Paris & Tokyo,** One of the finest of the new generation of Parisian chocolatiers, and member of l'Académie Française du Chocolat et de la Confiserie, Jean-Paul Hevin's chocolate boutiques are delicious invitations to the eyes as well as to the tongue. Below he shares with us a recipe for his popular old-fashioned chocolate macaroons.

## MACARON COOKIES

1. PLACE ALMONDS IN FOOD PROCESSOR OR BLENDER AND FINELY GRIND INTO A POWDER.

2. SIFT 1/5 CUP ALMOND POWDER, 5 TBS FINE GRANU-LATED SUGAR, AND 2 1/2 TBS WHITE FLOUR.

3. IN A BOWL, BEAT EGG WHITES UNTIL THEY ARE FIRM.

4. IN A SEPARATE BOWL, VIGOROUSLY WHISK 5 TBS OF STIFFLY BEATEN EGG WHITES AND 2 1/2 TBS FINE GRANULATED SUGAR.

5. INCORPORATE THE EGG AND SUGAR MIXTURE INTO THE ALMOND DOUGH.

6. COVER A BAKING TRAY WITH A COOKING SHEET. POUR COOKIE DOUGH INTO A PIPING BAG FITTED WITH A PIPING SOCKET (FOR EXAMPLE, A NO. 14 SOCKET) AND PIPE OUT PORTIONS OF THE DOUGH ONTO THE SHEET, FORMING CIRCLES (AS LARGE AS YOU WANT). YOU CAN ALSO USE A SPOON INSTEAD OF A PIPING BAG IF YOU WISH.

7. SPRINKLE CONFECTIONER'S SUGAR ON TOP OF THE COOKIE. COOK IN THE OVEN AT 355°F FOR 20 MINUTES.

## GANACHE

1. IN A SAUCEPAN, SLOWLY BRING CREAM AND COCOA POWDER TO BOILING.

2. POUR BOILING LIGHT CREAM AND COCOA POWDER ONTO GANACHE CHOCOLATE IN A SEPARATE BOWL.

3. WHEN THE CHOCOLATE HAS MELTED, STIR AND LEAVE THE GANACHE TO COOL.

4. STIR IN 9 TBS OF SOFTENED BUTTER.

## ASSEMBLY

1. PLACE ONE COOKIE ON THE TRAY, FLAT SIDE FACING UP, THEN ADD A LAYER OF GANACHE (1/2 INCH THICK), AND FINALLY ADD ON TOP A SECOND LAYER OF COOKIE (FLAT SIDE FACING DOWN).

2. REFRIGERATE FOR 12 HOURS

## MACARON COOKIES

1 CUP ALMONDS, TOASTED

7 1/2 TBS FINE GRANULATED SUGAR

2 1/2 TBS WHITE FLOUR

4 LARGE EGG WHITES

## GANACHE

1/2 CUP OF LIGHT CREAM

1/2 TBS COCOA POWDER

4.4 OZ. GANACHE CHOCOLATE, CHOPPED (USE BAKING CHOCOLATE WITH A REDUCED LEVEL OF COCOA BUTTER).

9 TBS SOFTENED BUTTER

3. OPTIONAL: USE THE SMALL AMOUNT OF GANACHE THAT IS LEFT OVER TO MAKE CHOCOLATE SHAVINGS. PRESS THE SHAVINGS ONTO VARIOUS PARTS OF THE CAKE.

## TO SERVE

TOP WITH CONFECTIONER'S SUGAR AND A SPRINKLING OF COCOA POWDER. THE KEY TO MAKING THIS RECIPE A SUCCESS IS TO USE GOOD EGG WHITES AND AN EXCELLENT COOKING TECHNIQUE. MAKES 4-5 SERVINGS

# DIPPED CAMEMBERT AND CHOCOLATE SANDWICH

Once Chef Philippe Jeanty of Napa Valley's Bistro Jeanty told us a story from his youth. He said, "My grandmother used to give me a snack coming back from school of bread, chocolate and camembert. It's a great taste sensation." Since then I've tried several ways to make the ultimate variation of this childhood delight. I think I've found it.

1. MELT CHOCOLATE. REMOVE FROM HEAT, AND SET ASIDE TO COOL.

2. SLICE THE BAGUETTE LENGTHWISE SO THAT IT OPENS INTO A SANDWICH.

3. CUT CAMEMBERT INTO SLICES APPROXIMATELY 1/3 TO 1/2 INCH THICKNESS. PREPARE ENOUGH SLICES SO THAT WHEN PLACED SIDE BY SIDE THEY WOULD FILL THE ENTIRE SANDWICH.

1 BAGUETTE, CUT TO APPROXIMATELY 9-INCHES IN LENGTH, OR TO A PREFERRED LENGTH

3 OZ. DARK CHOCOLATE

100 GRAMS OF CAMEMBERT

4. PUT EACH CAMEMBERT SLICE IN A SIEVE, PLACE OVER A BOWL, AND SPOON THE MELTED CHOCOLATE OVER THE CHEESE. OR IF YOU PREFER, YOU CAN PLACE EACH SLICE ON A SPATULA AND DIP IT INTO THE CHOCOLATE.

5. PUT CHOCOLATE COVERED CAMEMBERT SLICES ONTO A SHEET OF PARCHMENT OR WAX PAPER AND PLACE IN REFRIGERATOR FOR 30-45 MINUTES.

6. REMOVE CAMEMBERT FROM REFRIGERATOR AND PLACE SLICES IN A LINE INSIDE THE BAGUETTE. SERVES 1-2

VARIATION:

CHOP 1/2 CUP OF WALNUTS AND DRIZZLE OVER CAMEMBERT SLICES AFTER THEY'VE BEEN COATED WITH MELTED CHOCOLATE, THEN PLACE IN REFRIGERATOR TO SET.

# GRANDMOTHER'S CHOCOLATE MOUSSE

**Restaurant JEAN-LOUIS, Chef Jean-Louis Gerin, Greenwich, Connecticut,** "This is the first 'cooking' I was allowed to do when I was 8 years old. My grandmother showed me her recipe and I loved it so much I never changed it."

- 3 1/2 OZ. BITTER CHOCOLATE (75% CACAO), CHOPPED
- 7 OZ. SEMI-SWEET CHOCOLATE CHIPS (50% CACAO)
- 4 EGG YOLKS
- 1 1/2 CUPS EGG WHITES (8 EGG WHITES = 1 CUP)
- 1/2 CUP GRANULATED SUGAR

1. MELT BOTH CHOCOLATES TOGETHER. REMOVE FROM HEAT.

2. IN A BOWL, BEAT THE EGG YOLKS WITH 2 TABLESPOONS OF SUGAR UNTIL THE MIXTURE HAS A RIBBON-LIKE TEXTURE. THE BATTER SHOULD BE THICK AND DRIP FROM THE WHISK IN SMOOTH, THICK RIBBONS.

3. IN A SEPARATE BOWL, WHIP THE EGG WHITES, STARTING SLOWLY AND GRADUALLY INCREASING SPEED UNTIL THEY FORM A SOFT PEAK. ADD THE SUGAR SLOWLY AND FINISH WHIPPING UNTIL FIRM.

4. WHISK THE EGG YOLKS INTO THE CHOCOLATE, THEN ADD A THIRD OF THE EGG WHITE.

5. FINISH BY SLOWLY FOLDING THE REST OF THE EGG WHITE INTO THE CHOCOLATE.

6. REFRIGERATE OVERNIGHT.

## TO SERVE

SERVE WITH CAFE AU LAIT CRÈME ANGLAISE. MAKES 6 SERVINGS

## Chateau nougatine

Paroles: Roger Dumas. Musique: Jean-Jacques Debout

*[excerpt]*

Au chateau Nougatine,
Au chateau, miam! Miam! Miam!
Au chateau Nougatine,
Entrez messieurs, mesdames
Le chateau Nougatine,
Le chateau, miam! Miam! Miam!
Est un drole de chateau
Car c'est un gros gateau.

Tous les murs sont en genoise,
La toiture à la framboise.
Et sur son trône en bonbons,
Dans le salon calisson,
Si le roi est en nougat,
Les soldats en chocolat
On peut manger les fauteuils
car se sont des mille-feuilles.

*[translation]*

In the castle Nougatine,
In the castle, miam! Miam! Miam!
In the castle Nougatine,
Enter ladies and gentlemen
The castle Nougatine
The castle, miam! Miam! Miam!
It's a funny kind of castle
Because it's a great big cake.

All the walls are sponge cake
The roof is raspberry
And on his throne of candies
In the calisson great room
If the king is in nougat
The soldiers are in chocolate
We can eat up all the armchairs
'Cause they are mille-feuilles.

## LET THEM EAT CHOCOLATE

How do you keep a twelve-year-old chocoholic American happy in Paris: 1) Feed liberally with chocolate crêpes from any crêpe stand, 2) Add white chocolate golf balls from the famed Parisian chocolatier, Debauve et Gallais, 3) Finish with *truffes au chocolat* from La Maison de Chocolat. This formula makes my son smile with wistful happiness every time he remembers.

Chocolate snacks, chocolate shops, and chocolate desserts are everywhere you look in Paris. You can even get an entire chocolate brunch! Chocoholics of every age visiting Paris realize soon enough that they have arrived in *un paradis de chocolat*. From where does this French passion for chocolate come? It is in fact a taste that develops and is encouraged at the time *le jeune français* is in the cradle. An association of French pediatric nurses gives the following advice to young French mothers:

"Baby can begin to discover this new flavor at the age of six or seven months as chocolate cereal, then as cookies at about a year. Better to wait until 2 years of age for the first chocolate cakes... Chocolate is an essential virtue, the pleasure food par excellence. It is also a nutritious food which parents can give, within reason, to their petits gourmands in good conscience."

And so it begins. While the typical American mother cannot imagine choc-olate as a staple breakfast food, when many a French mother declares "*A table!* (Let's eat!)" to call her young ones to breakfast, it's likely they will be offered a steaming cup of hot chocolate and a pain au chocolat (chocolate-filled crois-sant). Breakfast is only the beginning of the chocolate-filled day of the French child. At the end of the long school day, which in France can continue until well after 4pm, what does the *jeune français* have for a snack upon arrival at home? *Plus de chocolat, bien sûr!* One of the most popular after-school snacks in France is a sandwich made with baguette slices encasing pieces of a choco-late bar. Of course this being France, there is much variety in taste. In some French homes, like that of my friend Bèatrice, the famous brand Nutella reigns supreme. This chocolate-and-hazelnut spread is slathered on baguettes to make another high-ranking snack, the "tartine." While a tartine literally refers to bread with any kind of spread, Nutella is by far one of the most popular choices for French kids. Fortunately, the spread is not just limited to topping a baguette. My friend Muriel fondly recalls her favorite childhood treat of crêpes heaped with Nutella. If you have a taste for such a delicacy, it's only as far away as your local crêpe stand.

Maybe this life-long taste for chocolate explains the general slimness of the French figure? Perhaps, or maybe not, but it seems to make *la vie française* a bit more enjoyable. That's why I suggest that regardless of your country of birth, whether you have a child, are a child-at-heart, or are simply an unabashed chocoholic, it's always a good idea to try to start or end your busy day the French child's way.

*Gerri Chanel*

## About GERRI CHANEL
Gerri Chanel is a French cooking instructor at the Alliance Française in Hartford, Connecticut. She has studied at the Cordon Bleu in Paris and has dined with Julia Child. Gerri is the editor of the newsletter, "A Table!," for lovers of French cuisine, wine and culture. She can be reached at gbc@atable.net.

## About l'alliance Française
The Alliance Française is one of several unique organizations the francophone or francophile can join. Founded in the 1880's, the Alliance is composed of a network of over 1,000 independently run committees in 130 countries.  With facilities in locations such as Paris, New York, San Francisco, Los Angeles, Toronto, Melbourne, Quito, London, Buenos Aires, and Miami, not only does it span geographic boundaries, but its services and programs are just as broad. As a non-profit French language school and a cultural center, the Alliance Française offers French classes several times a week at all levels of French proficiency, including subjects such as grammar, pronunciation, translation and conversation. The Alliance also presents exhibits, film festivals, literary discussions, wine tastings, cooking classes, and often in-house libraries and CD rentals.

# CHANEL'S CRÊPES

**Gerri Chanel, L'Alliance Française,** "This slightly-sweetened crêpe can serve as the base for an infinite number of desserts or snack fillings. Any kind of spread will work, from Nutella, chocolate or fruit jam to a simple sprinkling of sugar. If you are more ambitious, you can use any filling you can imagine: sweetened sliced peaches or strawberries and whipped cream, for example, or bananas sautéed in a little butter. For an even more decadent (and adult) dessert, reduce the water by a tablespoon or two and replace with Cognac or an orange-flavored liqueur such as Cointreau or Grand Marnier. Makes about ten crêpes using a skillet with an 8-inch diameter across the bottom"

1. COMBINE FLOUR, SUGAR, AND SALT IN A MEDIUM BOWL.

2. COMBINE EGGS AND YOLK IN A SEPARATE BOWL AND BEAT SLIGHTLY.

3. ADD THE EGGS, MILK, AND WATER TO THE DRY INGREDIENTS. USING A WHISK OR IN A BLENDER, BEAT UNTIL SMOOTH.

4. STIR IN THE MELTED BUTTER.

5. ALLOW THE BATTER TO REST IN THE REFRIGERATOR FOR AT LEAST ONE HOUR.

6. HEAT A SHALLOW-SIDED SKILLET, PREFERABLY NON-STICK, OVER MEDIUM-HIGH HEAT. THE PAN IS READY WHEN A DROP OF WATER SKITTERS ACROSS THE SURFACE. WHEN SKILLET IS HOT, ADD A SMALL AMOUNT OF BUTTER AND SWIRL AROUND THE PAN TO COAT THE BOTTOM.

7. POUR 1/4 CUP OF BATTER INTO PAN AND IMMEDIATELY AND QUICKLY TILT AND SWIRL THE PAN GENTLY IN A CIRCULAR MOTION TO EVENLY COAT THE BOTTOM. FOR LARGER PANS USE 1/2 CUP OF BATTER.

8. COOK CRÊPE ABOUT 1 MINUTE, OR UNTIL IT IS SET AND VERY SLIGHTLY BROWNED ON THE BOTTOM. FLIP CRÊPE AND COOK SECOND SIDE FOR ABOUT 30 SECONDS. THE SECOND SIDE WILL NOT BROWN AS NICELY AS THE FIRST SIDE. ADJUST THE HEAT AS NEEDED.

9. STACK AND COOL THE CRÊPES. IF NOT SERVING IMMEDIATELY, SEPARATE EACH CRÊPE WITH WAXED PAPER, WRAP, AND REFRIGERATE.

10. FILL THE FINISHED CRÊPES WITH DESIRED FILLING, THEN ROLL OR FOLD INTO QUARTERS, BROWNED-SIDE OUT.

3/4 CUP MILK

1/3 CUP WATER

2 EGGS

1 EGG YOLK

2 TBS BUTTER, MELTED (PLUS 2 MORE TBS FOR COATING PAN)

1 CUP FLOUR, ALL-PURPOSE

1 TBS SUGAR

A PINCH OF SALT

*A visitor tries chocolate crepes in Paris*

# CHOCOLATE AND VANILLA MADELEINES

Many people make chocolate Madeleines, where the entire tea cake is chocolate. As good as they are, it sometimes seems like overkill. Many things are often much more pleasurable when you leave a little to the imagination, partially covered, so to speak.

1. BUTTER THE INSIDE OF THE MADELEINE MOLDS, DUST WITH A BIT OF FLOUR, AND PLACE IN REFRIGERATOR TO CHILL.

2. MELT CHOCOLATE.

3. IN A SEPARATE SAUCEPAN, MELT 12 TBS OF BUTTER OVER MEDIUM HEAT FOR 4-6 MINUTES UNTIL IT IS LIGHTLY BROWNED (NOT BURNED). STIR OCCASIONALLY. REMOVE FROM HEAT.

4. PREHEAT OVEN TO 400ºF.

5. IN A BOWL, SIFT TOGETHER THE FLOUR AND SALT.

6. IN A SEPARATE BOWL, COMBINE SUGAR AND EGGS, AND WHIP EGGS UNTIL THEY BEGIN TO TURN A BIT WHITE AND THICKEN.

7. ADD FLOUR MIXTURE TO EGGS, AND FOLD TOGETHER. ADD MELTED BUTTER TO MIXTURE, STIR WELL.

8. DIVIDE THE RESULTING BATTER IN HALF, PUTTING HALF IN ANOTHER BOWL. IN ONE HALF ADD THE CHOCOLATE, IN THE OTHER HALF ADD THE VANILLA.

9. POUR THE BATTERS INTO THE MADELEINE MOLD. FILL 1/3 TO 1/2 OF EACH MOLD WITH THE CHOCOLATE BATTER, THEN ON TOP OF THE CHOCOLATE BATTER POUR THE VANILLA BATTER. STOP WHEN EACH MOLD IS 3/4 FULL, OR 1/4 FROM THE TOP OF THE MOLD.

10. PUT THE MADELEINE TIN IN THE OVEN FOR 10-15 MINUTES, UNTIL TOPS OF MADELEINES ARE A LIGHT GOLDEN BROWN AND THE MADELEINES ARE FIRM TO THE TOUCH (BUT NOT HARD TO THE TOUCH).

11. REMOVE FROM OVEN, TURN MOLDS UPSIDE DOWN AND REMOVE MADELEINES FROM THE MOLD. (IF NEEDED, RUN PARING KNIFE AROUND EDGE OF MOLD). PLACE ON A RACK OR TRAY TO COOL.

12. REPEAT WITH REMAINING BATTER IF DESIRED.

1 CUP OF ALL-PURPOSE FLOUR

3 OZ. OF BITTERSWEET CHOCOLATE

4 WHOLE EGGS

1 1/3 CUP OF SUGAR

2 TSP OF VANILLA EXTRACT

12 TBS OF BUTTER

PINCH OF SALT

BUTTER FOR MOLDS

SPECIAL EQUIPMENT:
MADELEINE MOLDS (TINS)

# CHOCOLATE CHIP MADELEINES

To get the most from this delight, be sure to use the best quality chocolate chips.

1. BUTTER THE INSIDE OF THE MADELEINE MOLDS, DUST WITH A BIT OF FLOUR, AND PLACE IN REFRIGERATOR TO CHILL.

2. IN A SEPARATE SAUCEPAN, MELT 12 TBS OF BUTTER OVER MEDIUM HEAT FOR 4-6 MINUTES UNTIL IT IS LIGHTLY BROWNED (NOT BURNED). STIR OCCASIONALLY. REMOVE FROM HEAT.

3. PREHEAT OVEN TO 400ºF.

4. IN A BOWL, SIFT TOGETHER THE FLOUR AND SALT.

5. IN A SEPARATE BOWL, COMBINE SUGAR AND EGGS, AND WHIP EGGS UNTIL THEY BEGIN TO TURN A BIT WHITE AND THICKEN.

6. ADD FLOUR MIXTURE TO EGGS, ADD VANILLA AND FOLD TOGETHER. ADD MELTED BUTTER TO MIXTURE, STIR WELL.

7. ADD CHOCOLATE CHIPS TO BATTER AND STIR WELL.

8. POUR THE BATTER INTO THE MADELEINE MOLD. STOP WHEN EACH INDIVIDUAL MOLD IS 3/4 FULL.

9. PUT THE MADELEINE TIN IN THE OVEN FOR 10-15 MINUTES, UNTIL TOPS OF MADELEINES ARE A LIGHT GOLDEN BROWN AND THE MADELEINES ARE FIRM TO THE TOUCH (BUT NOT HARD TO THE TOUCH).

10. REMOVE FROM OVEN, TURN MOLDS UPSIDE DOWN AND REMOVE MADELEINES FROM THE MOLD. PLACE ON A RACK OR TRAY TO COOL.

11. REPEAT IF DESIRED.

1 CUP OF ALL-PURPOSE FLOUR

1 CUP OF SEMISWEET CHOCOLATE CHIPS

4 WHOLE EGGS

1 CUP OF SUGAR

1 TSP OF VANILLA EXTRACT

12 TBS OF BUTTER

PINCH OF SALT

BUTTER FOR MOLDS

## SPECIAL EQUIPMENT:
MADELEINE MOLDS (TINS)

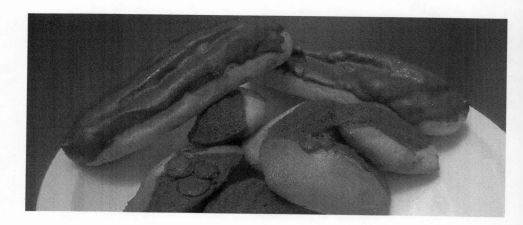

# MONIQUE'S CHOCOLATE BRIQUE

**Danielle Avidan, Los Angeles, Alliance Française,** "This is my good friend Monique's recipe. I met Monique over twenty years ago. She had recently inherited a beautiful house from her aunt in the La Rochelle region and was spending part of the year in France. I admired her a lot for her culture, her generosity, and the way she expressed herself without a word of 'franglais,' even though she had spent a lot of time on a U.S. base with her dentist husband. She was an inspired cook, knew how to make homemade 'rillettes' - and after dinner would send us home with care packages."

1. BREAK THE CHOCOLATE INTO PIECES AND PLACE IN A BOWL WITH ONE TABLESPOON OF COFFEE. MELT CHOCOLATE MIXTURE, THEN SET ASIDE TO COOL DOWN.

2. POUR THE REST OF THE COFFEE INTO A SHALLOW PAN.

3. DIP COOKIES INTO THE MIXTURE, BUT DO NOT ALLOW TO BECOME SOGGY.

4. LINE A COOKIE SHEET WITH FOIL. PLACE COOKIES IN A LINE OF SIX, CLOSE TO EACH OTHER. THIS FORMS THE FIRST LAYER.

5. SPREAD SOME CHOCOLATE OVER; THEN ADD A SECOND LAYER OF COOKIES, ANOTHER LAYER OF CHOCOLATE, ETC., UNTIL YOU HAVE FORMED THREE LAYERS OF COOKIES.

6. FINISH BY TOPPING WITH CHOCOLATE WHICH WILL RUN AND COVER THE SIDES. THUS A BRICK (BRIQUE) IS FORMED.

GARNISH THE TOP WITH ALMONDS. REFRIGERATE BEFORE SERVING.

1 PACKAGE OF 18 SHORT-BREAD COOKIES (RECTANGULAR OR SQUARE)

1 PINT STRONG COFFEE

8 OZ. BITTERSWEET CHOCOLATE

4 OZ. SOFTENED BUTTER

1 TBS ROASTED SLIVERED ALMONDS

*Danielle Avidan*

*This Page:* The selections at Pierre Chauvet Artisan Chocolatier 32, Avenue Victor Hugo, Aubenas (France) and 3, Place des Clercs, Valence (France)

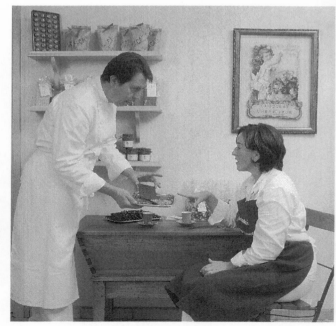

Above: The selections at Chocolats Girard, 4, rue des Archives, Paris (France), Below: The delicious Truffettes de France

# RED FRUIT, CHOCOLATE & VANILLA CLAFOUTIS

Clafoutis were originally made in the Limoges region with seasonal cherries, but now you can find just about anything in them, including savory meats and vegetables. Pears and apples are two of the most common substitutes. The recipe here is for a delicious clafoutis that uses what the French call, "fruit rouges," which as it says are "red fruits." In this case the red fruits are strawberries, cherries, and raspberries. Combined with semi-sweet chocolate, the dish is difficult to resist, or forget.

1. PREHEAT OVEN TO 350ºF.

2. BUTTER THE INSIDE OF AN OVEN-PROOF BAKING DISH.

3. COMBINE CHOCOLATE, BUTTER AND MILK IN A SAUCEPAN OVER LOW HEAT. STIR SLOWLY UNTIL CHOCOLATE IS MELTED. REMOVE PAN FROM HEAT AND LET CHOCOLATE MIXTURE COOL.

4. PLACE THE SLICED RED FRUIT ACROSS THE BOTTOM OF THE BAKING DISH, EVENLY DISTRIBUTING THE FRUIT PIECES.

5. IN A BOWL, COMBINE THE SUGAR, EGGS AND VANILLA. GENTLY WHIP UNTIL THE SUGAR IS DISSOLVED.

6. ADD THE FLOUR INTO THE EGGS, GENTLY STIRRING UNTIL THE FLOUR IS FULLY INCORPORATED INTO THE BATTER.

7. POUR THE MELTED CHOCOLATE MIXTURE INTO THE EGG BATTER. MIX WELL.

8. POUR THE EGG AND CHOCOLATE BATTER INTO THE BAKING DISH. IF THE FRUIT MOVES, USE A SPOON TO REPOSITION PIECES SO THAT THEY ARE EVENLY DIS-TRIBUTED.

9. PLACE IN OVEN FOR 30-40 MINUTES, UNTIL THE TOP IS A GOLDEN BROWN AND THE CUSTARD IS SET.

3 1/2 OZ. OF SEMI-SWEET CHOCOLATE, CHOPPED

1 1/3 CUP OF MILK

4 CUPS RASPBERRIES, STRAW-BERRIES, & CHERRIES, SLICED IN HALVES AND PITTED

4 EGGS

3/4 CUP OF SUGAR

4 TSP OF VANILLA EXTRACT

3/4 CUP OF FLOUR

3 TBS BUTTER

BUTTER FOR THE DISH

## TO SERVE

MAY BE SERVED WARM WITH A SIDE OF VANILLA ICE CREAM
SERVES 6

# Chocolate Sorbet

**Le Zinc, Chef Max Braud, San Francisco,** This sorbet is an excellent and tasty example of the results of combining a few basic ingredients with a simple French touch.

1. Pour water into a pan and add sugar.
2. Heat gently until the sugar has completely dissolved, stirring from time to time.
3. Break dark chocolate into small pieces and place in a bowl over a bain-marie (or double-boiler) to melt.
4. When the chocolate has melted mix it with a wooden spatula. Add sifted cocoa powder and mix carefully.
5. Pour the warm syrup over the chocolate mixture, stirring constantly.
6. Leave to cool and then place in a sorbet machine. Place in freezer until set.

Recipe is for 1 litre of sorbet.

6 1/2 oz. of dark chocolate

4 Tbs of cocao powder

3/4 cup of granulated sugar

2 1/2 cups water

### Special equipment
sorbet machine

### La Maison du Chocolat

*225, rue du Faubourg Saint-Honoré, Paris*
*also in New York, Tokyo, and other locations*

Chocolate can be made into many things, but a chocolate house would not last very long, especially one made of the finest French chocolate and the most delectable designs. With this inescapable reality in mind, La Maison du Chocolat has instead focused on great truffles and macaroons made of chocolate. The results are quite tasteful, and tasty.

# FRENCH CHOCOLATE IN FILM

Filmmakers have long used chocolate as a symbol of smoldering desire, especially in their movie titles. We recommend six movies that use French chocolate as either a unifying theme or a figurative allusion.

### Merci pour le Chocolat (2000)
Directed by Claude Chabrol
Starring: Isabelle Huppert, Jacques Dutronc, Anna Mouglalis, Rodolphe Pauly

Isabelle Huppert plays Milka Muller, a melancholy woman who runs the prosperous chocolate business inherited from her father. Though she is unmoved by the workings of the chocolate business, in the kitchen she is inspired by chocolate almost to the point of fanaticism. Her husband is André, a pianist whose wife died in a car accident years before. Their 18 year old son has neither interest nor talent in playing the piano. One day, a talented 18 year old piano student comes to visit. She claims to be Andre's daughter, switched at the hospital at birth.... the secret is revealing.

"A subtle, unnerving performance from Isabelle Huppert enlivens Claude Chabrol's elegantly creepy thriller," says Peter Bradshaw of London newspaper, The Guardian. "Claude Chabrol's sinuous little thriller, for all its flaws, is a welcome... imaginative response to the sensuality of chocolate: delicious, but dark and bitter.

**Sex & Chocolate (1997, BBC TV)**
Directed by Gavin Millar
Starring: Dawn French

Dawn French stars as Bev Bodger, a married teacher who is tempted by an old school boyfriend to enjoy a little sex and chocolate in Paris.

**Hot Chocolate (1992)**
alternate title in France, **Amour et chocolat**
Directed by Josee Dayan
Starring: Bo Derek, Vincent Cassel

B.J. Cassidy, a rich businesswoman, has to invest several billion dollars for fiscal reasons. She undertakes to buy back a small French factory, specializing in chocolate truffles.

**Pain au chocolat (1998)**
alternate title, **Plain or Chocolate**
Directed by Didier Blasco

**Chocolat amer (1993)**
alternate title, **Bitter Chocolate**
Directed by Isabelle Broue

**La Bombe au chocolat (1997)**
Directed by Sylvie Rosenthal

**Chocolat**
Directed by Claire Denis
A woman remembers her young years as a French colonialist in Africa, and the relationships she had while there.

*Dijon, Capital of the Burgundy region*

## "CHOCOLAT"

The French love the cinema as much, if not more, than almost any other country. This love partially explains the continued vibrancy and endurance of France's domestic film & entertainment industry, even when faced with the flood of movies and television shows generated by Hollywood.

Ironically, the power of the cinema has had a profound influence on the appreciation of the relationship between French culture and chocolate. In the year 2000, the movie "Chocolat" was released to the world. The movie, starring actors Juliette Binoche, Johnny Depp, Alfred Molina, Carrie-Anne Moss, and Judi Dench, created a revolution in the appreciation for the magic of chocolate. In the film, a mother (Binoche) and her daughter arrive in a rural town in France, where they open a small chocolate shop across the street from the local church and the office of the Mayor. The Mayor, the Comte de Reynaud, a descendant of the local aristocracy, objects to the sinful presence of the chocolate shop and the woman in his pious community. The woman however has different plans, and uses chocolate to unlock the secret hopes, dreams and passions of the townspeople. Shot in French locations such as Dijon and Flavigny-sur-Ozcrain, the film revitalized chocolate sales not just in the United States, England and Australia, but in France as well.

*Let me put this in perspective for you. The first Comte de Reynaud expelled all the radical Huguenots in this village. You and your truffles present a far lesser challenge.*
    **- Comte de Reynaud , scene from the film, "Chocolat"**

*I have always loved chocolate but in CHOCOLAT, chocolate becomes more than just a sweet taste. It becomes a gesture towards others or towards yourself, a sort of compassion. It is a wonderful symbol for the exchange of gifts, emotions, honesty, and caring between people*
    **- Juliette Binoche, about the film, "Chocolat"**

*To me, CHOCOLAT is a very funny fable about temptation and the importance of not denying oneself the good things in life*
    **- Lasse Hallstrom, Director of "Chocolat"**

# LAMB WITH DARK CHOCOLATE SAUCE

In a very memorable scene in the film "Chocolat," Juliette Binoche prepares a feast for ailing friend Judi Dench. Every dish in the feast, from lamb to chicken, was bathed in dark chocolate. The recipe we've included of the lamb dish is not as rich, but is just as delicious. It is based on a recipe for celebrated French chef Guy Martin's famous rack of lamb with chocolate sauce. We prefer to start with a pre-prepared lamb stock, purchased at a gourmet food store. We also include more chocolate in the sauce.

1. TRIM RACK OF ANY REMAINING FAT.

2. MELT THE CHOCOLATE. REMOVE FROM HEAT.

3. HEAT THE LAMB STOCK TO A LOW SIMMER AND ADD 1 TSP OF CHOCOLATE, FOLLOWED BY WHISKING THE BUTTER INTO THE SAUCE. ADD FENNEL SEEDS, SALT, AND PEPPER. REMOVE FROM HEAT.

4. PREHEAT THE OVEN TO 400ºF.

5. PEEL AND CUT GRAPES IN HALF. REMOVE ANY SEEDS.

6. IN A BOWL, COMBINE BLUEBERRY PRESERVES AND DIJON MUSTARD. MIX WELL.

7. IN A PAN OVER MEDIUM-HIGH HEAT, QUICKLY BROWN EACH LAMB RACK ON BOTH SIDES, THEN BASTE THEM WITH THE BLUEBERRY PRESERVES AND DIJON MUSTARD.

8. REMOVE LAMB FROM PAN, PLACE IN OVEN, BASTE, THEN COOK FOR 10-12 MINUTES. REMOVE FROM OVEN AND ALLOW RACKS TO REST FOR 10 MINUTES. CUT APART EACH RIB FROM THE RACKS OF LAMB SO THAT THEY MAKE INDIVIDUAL CHOPS.

## TO SERVE

ARRANGE LAMB CHOPS ON PLATES, DRIZZLE WITH SAUCE AND ADD THE GRAPES AROUND THE EDGE OF THE PLATES. SERVES 4

- 2 RACKS OF LAMB, RIB CUT, CLEANED OF FAT, WITH AT LEAST SIX RIBS EACH
- 4 TBS BLUEBERRY PRESERVES
- 1 TBS DIJON-STYLE MUSTARD
- 8 WHITE GRAPES
- 1.75 OZ. OF CHOPPED DARK CHOCOLATE
- 3/4 OZ. BUTTER
- 5 FENNEL SEEDS, (OR BLACK CUMIN)
- SALT AND PEPPER TO TASTE
- 1 1/2 CUP LAMB STOCK

# CHOCOLATE MOUSSE

**Le Zinc, Chef Max Braud, San Francisco**, According to chef-owner Max Braud, "There is almost nothing more satisfying than the pairing of a fine red French wine with pure dark chocolate. This pairing idea is contrary to the belief that chocolate and a dessert wine go well together. The tannins in the red wine enhance the taste of the bitter-sweetness of the chocolate." With this revolutionary idea in mind, a good red with this mousse makes a unique finish to a meal.

1. BREAK THE CHOCOLATE INTO SMALL PIECES AND MELT (PER PAGE 28).

2. BEAT THE EGG WHITES WITH A PINCH OF SALT. WHEN THE VOLUME STARTS TO INCREASE ADD HALF OF THE SUGAR. WHEN THE WHITES STIFFEN ADD THE REST OF THE SUGAR SLOWLY AND CONTINUE BEATING ON HIGH SPEED UNTIL STIFF AND FLUFFY.

3. ADD THE BUTTER TO THE MELTED CHOCOLATE AND MIX WELL.

4. NOW THE MIXTURE HAS COOLED DOWN MIX IN THE EGG YOLKS.

5. ADD THE BEATEN EGG WHITE MIXTURE TO THE CHOCOLATE MIXTURE. COMBINE A LITTLE AT A TIME USING A SPATULA TO FOLD THE MIXTURES GENTLY WITHOUT BREAKING DOWN THE BEATEN EGG WHITES.

6. WHEN THE MIXTURE IS COMPLETELY SMOOTH, POUR THE MIXTURE INTO BOWLS AND REFRIGERATE FOR 3-6 HOURS. SERVES 10

**6 EGG WHITES**

**4 EGG YOLKS**

**9 OZ. BITTER CHOCOLATE**

**3 1/2 TBS BUTTER**

**1/4 CUP GRANULATED SUGAR (SUPERFINE)**

**A PINCH OF SALT**

# CHOCOLATE PAVÉ

**Valencia Chocolates, Chef Rob Valencia, New York,** "A favorite confection that I enjoyed in France is what is called Pavé. Simple squares of chocolate ganache that are dusted in cocoa. Very rich and elegant, more so that just a simple truffle."

1. MELT CHOCOLATE TOGETHER.

2. IN BOWL, WHIP SUGAR AND YOLKS USING A MIXER UNTIL LIGHT AND RIBBONY.

3. ADD CREAM, BUTTER INTO SAUCEPAN. SPLIT AND SCRAPE THE VANILLA BEAN AND ADD TO CREAM. BRING TO A BOIL. REMOVE FROM HEAT.

4. POUR CREAM MIXTURE INTO YOLK/SUGAR MIXTURE. WHIP WITH THE MIXER AT LOW SPEED UNTIL COOL

5. STRAIN CREAM, SUGAR AND YOLK MIXTURE INTO THE MELTED CHOCOLATES AND WHISK UNTIL SMOOTH AND VELVETY.

6. POUR PAVÉ BATTER ON WAX PAPER AND LET SPREAD OUT INTO A THIN LAYER, OR POUR IN AN ACETATE LINED SHEET PAN. TAPS SIDE OF PAN TO ENSURE A FULL SPREAD.

7. CHILL UNTIL FIRM.

8. USING A HOT KNIFE CUT INTO SYMMETRICAL SQUARES ABOUT 1/2 INCH EACH.

9. DIP IN A BOWL OF COCOA AND SHAKE OFF EXCESS. KEEP IN COOL PLACE. MAKES 36 PIECES

**10 PASTEURIZED EGG YOLKS***

**10 TBS SUGAR**

**1 1/4 CUPS CREAM**

**1 1/4 CUPS BUTTER**

**1 WHOLE VANILLA BEAN**

**32 OZ. BITTERSWEET, MELTED**

**32 OZ. MILK CHOCOLATE, MELTED**

**2 CUPS POWDERED COCOA**

***NOTE ON PASTEURIZED YOLKS: PASTEURIZED YOLKS ARE A TYPE OF EGG THAT WHILE STILL TECHNICALLY RAW, HAS BEEN BROUGHT TO A POINT OF PASTEURIZATION IN WHICH THE BACTERIA ARE KILLED AND IT IS SAFE TO USE, YET REMAINS "UNCOOKED."**

## WEST COAST CHOCOLATE SALON EVENTS

In the summer of 2007, TasteTV and its Chocolate Television program organized the first major chocolate show on the West Coast in two decades. The San Francisco International CHOCOLATE SALON was held on Bastille Day Weekend, July 14 and 15, 2007 in San Francisco. Chocolate aficionados, fanatics, buyers and journalists experienced the finest in artisan, gourmet & premium chocolate in one of the world's great culinary metropolitan areas.

This first Salon drew over 2,000 attendees over the weekend, and highlights featured chocolate tasting, demonstrations, chef & author talks, wine pairings, chocolate painting, a chocolate spa and makeovers, and ongoing interviews by TasteTV's Chocolate Television program.

This event marked the launch of TasteTV's chocolate lifestyle brand, ChocolateTelevision.com. The launch included large and small scale Chocolate Salons in cities nationwide such as San Francisco, Los Angeles, Napa, Las Vegas, Seattle, Miami, and New York. It also began the broadcast of Chocolate Television, as well as the publication of books such as "Chocolate French," and "The Chocolate Guide: To Chocolatiers, Chocolate Makers, Boutiques, Patisseries and Shops"

TasteTV's West Coast Chocolate Salons are now major annual components of the *Chocolate Lifestyle* and *Francais au Chocolat*.

## FRENCH CHICAGO

Chicago has long been known as a culinary haven, and its French roots run very deep. Chicago, in fact, was founded by French-Haitian trader, fur trapper, farmer, and businessman Jean Baptiste Point du Sable in 1779 at the mouth of the Chicago river. His trading post was made up of a mill, bakehouse, dairy, smokehouse, workshop, poultry house, horse stable, and a barn, and was a major supply station for pioneers on the frontier as well as for Native Americans. Since that time the French influence has ebbed and flowed, culminating in a number of fantastic restaurants and cultural institutions. Three such places are Café Matou, Carlos', and the French Pastry School.

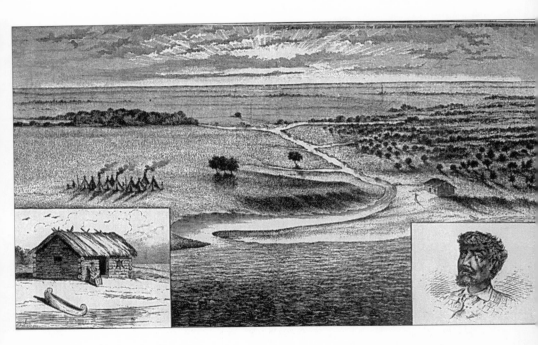

*French-Haitian trader, fur trapper, farmer, and businessman Jean Baptiste Point du Sable in 1779*

# WARM CHOCOLATE CAKE WITH CHANTILLY CRÈME AND RASPBERRY SAUCE

**Carlos', Highland Park, Illinois**, Carlos' specializes in contemporary French dishes, such as poached breast of pheasant and venison loin crusted in cocoa powder. For over two decades the restaurant has been located in Highland Park, an upscale suburb on Chicago's North Shore, where the residents are very exacting of taste, perfection, and authenticity. Carlos' has received awards from several notable sources, including Gourmet and Wine Spectator magazines, as well as the Zagat guide. Owners Carlos and Debbie Nieto say that this warm chocolate cake is a local favorite.

## WARM CHOCOLATE CAKE

1. PREHEAT OVEN TO 350°F.
2. COMBINE THE CHOCOLATE AND BUTTER AND MELT. WHISK WELL.
3. IN A BOWL, WHISK TOGETHER THE EGGS, POWDERED SUGAR, ESPRESSO AND VANILLA.
4. MIX MELTED CHOCOLATE & BUTTER INTO THE EGG MIXTURE.
5. SHIFT TOGETHER THE FLOUR, COCOA, AND BAKING POWDER.
6. ADD DRY FLOUR MIXTURE TO THE MELTED CHOCOLATE AND EGGS
7. TO BAKE, TAKE ONE LARGE 8 OR 9-INCH, GREASE PAN AND LINE WITH PARCHMENT PAPER AND POUR BATTER INTO THE ROUND. ALLOW 30 MINUTES BAKING TIME. IDEALLY, THE CAKE'S CENTER REMAINS "OOZY".

NOTE: IF YOU BAKE THIS BATTER IMMEDIATELY, PLEASE BE AWARE THAT IT WILL "SOUFFLÉ. IN OTHER WORDS, THE CAKE WILL RISE TO AN AMAZING HEIGHT AND UPON COOLING WILL FALL NOTICEABLY.

## CHANTILLY CREME

COMBINE INGREDIENTS AND WHIP CRÈME TO STIFF PEAKS.

## RASPBERRY SAUCE

1. COMBINE INGREDIENTS IN A POT AND BRING TO A BOIL.
2. LOWER HEAT AND ALLOW TO REDUCE TO SAUCE-LIKE CONSISTENCY.
4. STRAIN SAUCE AND ALLOW TO COOL.

## TO SERVE

POSSIBLE ACCOMPANIMENTS RECOMMEND BY CHEF:
    FRUIT, ICE CREAM, SORBET, WHIPPED CREAM, SAUCES.

## WARM CHOCOLATE CAKE

11 OZ. SEMI-SWEET CHOCOLATE

10 OZ. BUTTER, UNSALTED

1 CUP POWDERED SUGAR (NOT PACKED)

3/4 CUP ESPRESSO

1 TSP VANILLA EXTRACT

5 WHOLE EGGS

2/3 CUP FLOUR, ALL-PURPOSE

1/8 CUP COCOA POWDER, UNSWEETENED

1 1/4 TSP BAKING POWDER

## CHANTILLY CREME

1 1/2 CUP HEAVY WHIPPING CREAM

1 1/2 TBS POWDERED SUGAR

1 TSP VANILLA

## RASPBERRY SAUCE

1 PINT RASPBERRIES, FRESH OR FROZEN

1/2 CUP SUGAR

1/4 CUP WATER

A SQUEEZE OF LEMON JUICE

RASPBERRY COULIS WORKS QUITE NICELY WITH THE CAKE. SERVES 6-8

# Phyllo Cups with Chocolate Mousse, Raspberries and Poached Pears

**Cafe Matou, Chef Charlie Socher, Chicago,** A native Chicagoan and a former professor of economics at the University of Alaska, Chef Charlie Socher moved to Paris in 1981 to pursue his cooking career. After completing culinary apprenticeships in France, including those at two Michelin-rated restaurants, Au Quai des Ormes and Jacques Cogna, Socher returned to Chicago. His first head chef position was at The Chardonnay, which earned 3 1/2 stars from the Chicago Tribune. Prior to opening Cafe Matou in late 1997, Socher served as chef at other Chicago restaurants including Chezz Chazz, Brett's and Zaven's.

## Phyllo Cups

1. Preheat oven to 375ºF.
2. Butter 4 cups in a 12-cup muffin pan. (Do not butter adjacent cups.)
3. Stack phyllo sheets; cut in half cross-wise to form 12 rectangles.
4. Place 1 phyllo rectangle on work surface.
5. Cover remaining phyllo with plastic wrap and a damp cloth to prevent drying.
6. Brush phyllo with melted butter then sprinkle with 1/2 tablespoon each of sugar and almonds.
7. Place a second phyllo rectangle on top of first, brush with butter and sprinkle with 1/2 table-spoon each of sugar and almonds.
8. Repeat 3 more times and top with 1 more phyllo sheet and brush with butter. Phyllo stack will consist of 6 rectangles.
9. Cut out two 6-inch round phyllo stacks; use a sharp knife and a round plate as a guide.
10. Repeat the above phyllo stacking procedure with the remaining phyllo to make 4.
11. Bake phyllo cups for 10 minutes or until golden.
12. Quickly, and with a gentle twist, remove phyllo cups from pan.
13. Cook completely on a wire rack.
14. Store at room temperature in an air-tight container for up to two days.

## Phyllo Cups

6 fresh phyllo pastry sheets or frozen, thawed (approximately 17 x 13 inches each)

7 Tbs unsalted butter, melted

5 Tbs granulated sugar

5 Tbs finely chopped almonds

## Chocolate Mousse

3 1/2 oz. semisweet chocolate

2 Tbs cocoa

5 Tbs unsalted butter, room temperature

2 large eggs, separated

1 1/2 tsp granulated sugar

4 1/2 Tbs heavy cream, whipped

## Fruit Topping

1/2 pint fresh raspberries

2 pears, poached & diced

## Chocolate mousse

1. Melt chocolate and 1 tablespoon of butter. Remove from heat to cool.
2. Mix together into a cream the remaining butter and egg yolks, adding one yolk at a time.
3. Add two tablespoons of cocoa to the butter and egg yolk mixture.
4. Combine melted chocolate mixture with egg yolk mixture.
5. Whip egg whites with sugar to soft peaks and fold into above mixture. Fold in whipped cream.
6. Cover and chill until set (at least 3 hours) or overnight.

## Assembly of Filled Phyllo Cups

1. Fill phyllo cups with chocolate mousse.
2. Top with raspberries and pears. Serves 4

# BANANA PEARL

**French Pastry School, Chef Jacquy Pfeiffer & Chef Sebastien Canonne, Chicago,** Chef Jacquy Pfeiffer is a Master Pastry Chef who managed and coached the 2002 World Pastry Champion team and was honored with the prestigious Jean Banchet Award for Best Culinary School. The French Pastry School's other co-founder is Chef Sebastien Canonne, who apprenticed at the renowned Paris pastry shop, Gaston Lenotre, followed by time at the famous La Cote St. Jacques Restaurant in Burgundy alongside three-star Michelin Chef Michel Lorain. He and Chef Pfeiffer named as two of the Top Ten Pastry Chefs in the United States by both Chocolatier and Pastry Art & Design magazines in both 1996 and 1997.

## SACHER BISCUIT

1 CUP ALMOND PASTE 60/40

1/4 CUP GRANULATED SUGAR

3/4 CUP EGG YOLKS

1/2 CUP WHOLE EGGS

3/4 CUP EGG WHITES

1/4 TSP EGG WHITE POWDER

1/2 CUP SUGAR

1/4 TSP SALT

1/2 CUP CAKE FLOUR

1/4 CUP COCOA POWDER

1/4 CUP (4 TBS) BUTTER, MELTED

1/4 CUP COCOA PASTE

## GANACHE

1/2 CUP DARK CHOCOLATE (70% CACAO)

4 1/2 TBS WHOLE MILK

3/4 TBS CREAM AT 35%

1/4 CUP PLUGRA BUTTER 82%

## CARAMELIZED BANANAS

12 BANANAS

1/2 CUP SUGAR

1/4 CUP BUTTER

1/8 TSP NUTMEG

3 TSP LEMON JUICE

A PINCH OF SALT

## CHOCOLATE GLAZE

1 1/8 CUP MILK

1/2 CUP GLUCOSE

4 LEAVES GELATIN, PRESOAKED IN COLD WATER AND SQUEEZED OF EXCESS WATER

10.5 OZ. (300G, 1 CUP) WHITE CHOCOLATE

10.5 OZ. (300G, 1 CUP) WHITE PÂTE À GLACER (BAKER'S COVERING CHOCOLATE)

## RICE KRISPIES CRISP

1 1/2 TSP MILK CHOCOLATE, COUVERTURE QUALITY

1/2 CUP HAZELNUT PRALINE (MADE WITH 1 CUP SUGAR, 1 CUP HAZELNUTS, 6 TBS WATER, SEE BELOW)

2 1/2 CUP "RICE KRISPIES" BRAND CEREAL (OR OF SIMILAR DESIGN)

1/4 CUP ROASTED CHOPPED ALMONDS

## VANILLA BAVARIAN

1/2 CUP WATER

1 WHOLE VANILLA BEAN

1/4 CUP + 2 1/2 TBS SUGAR

1/4 CUP TRIMOLINE

1 1/4 CUP HEAVY CREAM

1 1/4 CUP MILK

3/4 CUPS EGG YOLKS

7 LEAVES GELATIN (SOAKED IN COLD WATER AND SQUEEZED OF EXCESS WATER)

1/4 CUP + 2 1/2 TBS WATER

3 CUPS WHIPPED CREAM

## Sacher Biscuit

1. Mix the first four ingredients (almond paste, egg yolks, whole eggs, sugar) and whisk until they have a ribbon-like texture. The batter should be thick and drip from the whisk in smooth, thick ribbons.
2. Make a soft meringue with the next four ingredients. First whisk the egg whites, egg powder and salt in a bowl until they have peaks, then whisk in half of the sugar, and fold in the other half
3. Fold half of the meringue into the egg mixture.
4. Fold in the sifted flour and cocoa powder.
5. Fold in the remaining meringue.
6. Fold in the melted butter and melted cocoa paste.
7. Pour the batter into two 8-inch cake circles.
8. Bake the biscuit at 350°F for 35 minutes. Demold the biscuit and wrap in a towel. Freeze.

## Ganache

1. Chop the chocolate into pieces. Make sure chocolate is at room temperature. Place pieces in a bowl.
2. Bring the milk and cream to a boil in a saucepan.
3. Pour the milk and cream over the chopped chocolate, and let the mixture stand until the chocolate ganache has cooled at 104°F.
4. Incorporate all the ingredients of the ganache with a whisk from the center out.
5. When the ganache is at 96.8°F mix a small amount of ganache with the butter, then fold the butter with the rest of the ganache.

## Caramelized Bananas

1. Slice the bananas and mix with the lemon juice.
2. In a pan, melt the butter over medium heat for 4-6 minutes until it is lightly browned (not burned). Stir occasionally. Remove from heat.
3. Add the bananas, sugar and nutmeg to the pan of butter, turn back on heat, and sauté the bananas until they are nicely caramelized and have a golden or dark brown coating.

## Chocolate Glaze

1. Bring milk and glucose to a boil.
2. Add soaked gelatin.
3. Pour over melted chocolate when mixture is at 100ºF.
4. Blend with a hand blender until smooth.
5. Refrigerate, then use at 85ºF.

## Rice Krispies Crisp

1. To make praline: Add sugar, water, and hazelnuts to a saucepan, and bring to a boil. Stir frequently until boiling, then do not stir.
2. Let continue to boil until syrup is a medium golden caramel color and the hazelnuts begin to pop.
3. Pour praline onto parchment lined baking sheet and allow to cool. Do not under any circumstance touch or taste the caramel until completely cooled - mixture is extremely hot on bare skin.
4. When cooled, break praline into small pieces using a blender, food processor, or rolling pin.

5. To temper chocolate couverture, melt chocolate in bowl, stirring frequently but not continuously. Remove from heat. When chocolate has cooled, reheat for about 1-2 minutes.

6. Mix all of the ingredients together and divide into two 8-inch flexipans. Let set.

## Vanilla Bavarian

1. Split the vanilla bean in half.

2. Bring the water, vanilla, sugar, and trimoline to a boil. Remove from heat. Let the mixture sit for 15 minutes and blend in a robot coupe (or blender).

3. Mix the vanilla infusion with the cream and milk and bring to a boil.

4. Add the egg yolks and cook to 160ºF.

5. Add the gelatin and cool over an ice bath.

6. Fold in the whipped cream when the Bavarian is at 90°F.

## To Assemble

1. Build the cake upside down.

2. Place two 8-inch rings on a plastic sheet.

3. Line the rings with acetate strips.

4. Place a layer of vanilla bavarian in the ring and allow it to thicken.

5. Place the caramelized bananas onto the bavarian.

6. Place the layer of the crisp on it.

7. Spread the ganache on the biscuit.

8. Place the biscuit on the crisp.

9. Freeze for 6 hours.

10. Unmold the cake and glaze it with the chocolate glaze.

11. Decorate the cake with chocolate shavings.

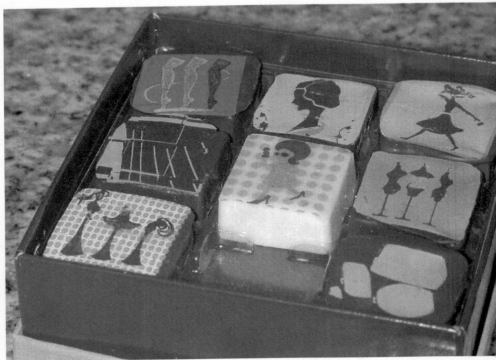

*Opposite Page: Mariebelle Chocolates, New York*

*This Page: Cocoa Bella Chocolates, San Francisco*

# La Rousse au chocolat
### Jacques Higelin

*[excerpt]*

J'ouvre un magazine et je vois
Une jolie p'tite rousse
Qui s'tape une mousse au chocolat
Ses lèvres gourmandes
M'invitent à en prendre avec elle
Rien qu'une cuillère
Avant qu'sa grandmère
Ne revienne

*[translation]*

I open a magazine and I see
A pretty little redhead
putting away a chocolate mousse
Her gourmand lips
Invite me to have some with her
Just a spoonful
Before her grandmother
Comes back home

Publisher's Note:
In the hope that
New Orleans will be
rebuilt and return
to its former glory,
the New Orleans
section of this book
has not been
removed or edited
since Hurricane
Katrina. Some
featured
restaurants may
have changed or
been permanently
closed since that
unfortunate event.

# FRENCH NEW ORLEANS

A wonderland of jazz, food, and French language, New Orleans and southern Louisiana are fascinating cultural puzzles. The region originally belonged to Native Americans, then to various European colonists such as the Spanish and the French, as well as to the Yankees who eventually annexed it to the Union. If this were ancient Phoenicia or Egypt, one would be able to dig into the earth and find layers of civilization upon civilization, neatly organized for archeologists to discover. But the moist, spongy soil in this part of the world doesn't play by those rules. Indeed, it will not tolerate any long-term human artifact or remnant, even those as common as graves, which explains why cemeteries in New Orleans are above ground.

There are two major types of French-influenced cuisine in New Orleans. The first is Creole, the second is Cajun. Creoles originally were French settlers, usually sons of French aristocrats who came to America to seek their fortune. In general, the term "Creole" tended to refer to local-born French colonists versus France-born French. Later it also referred to people of mixed descent, in particular those with African roots.

Creole is said to be the "food of the city," having more elements of African and Spanish influences, and Cajun is said to be the "food of the country." Cajuns, or *Acadians*, are descendants of French settlers forcefully expelled from Nova Scotia by the British in 1755, migrating subsequently to French-friendly Louisiana. There they adapted to the new land and resources, while keeping elements of their old French dialect and society. Though Napoleon eventually sold Louisiana to the United States in one of history's largest real estate deals, the Cajuns and other French colonists remained. Adding further spice to the French influence in Louisiana were the people, both black and white, who sought refuge from the turmoil and revolutionary battles for liberty that took place in the former colony of *St. Domingue* (now Haiti).

Such is a small part of the history of New Orleans and Louisiana, a history as rich as that of ancient Phoenicia. One of the best known of these riches is the cuisine, and from both Creole and Cajun cultures come specialties such as gumbo, Jambalaya, shrimp etoufée, and fantastic bread pudding.

# PINK POODLE

**Zoe Bistro,  W Hotel New Orleans,** When the jet-setting W Hotel chain came to New Orleans, Zoe Bistro wasn't far behind. Now the restaurant is a modern Gallic centerpiece in French-loving southern Louisiana. The Pink Poodle shows the excitement you can create with hazelnut paste, some meringue, and 21 ounces of chocolate.

## HAZELNUT CRUNCH BASE

1. MELT CHOCOLATE AND PRALINOSA OVER A DOUBLE BOILER. REMOVE FROM HEAT AND ADD CRUSHED WAFERS. POUR A 1/4-INCH THICK LAYER OF THE MIXTURE ONTO A SHEET PAN, SPREAD EVENLY. REFRIGERATE UNTIL SET, ABOUT 15 MINUTES.

2. REMOVE FROM REFRIGERATOR. USING A COOKIE CUTTER, CUT OUT A 4-INCH DISC.

## CHOCOLATE MOUSSE

1. MELT CHOCOLATE.

2. WHIP EGG WHITES.

3. IN A SEPARATE BOWL, WHIP CREAM UNTIL IT FORMS SOFT PEAKS.

4. ADD EGG YOLKS INTO CHOCOLATE.

5. FOLD WHIPPED EGG WHITES INTO CHOCOLATE MIXTURE, THEN FOLD IN WHIPPED CREAM. SPREAD EVENLY IN A 1-INCH THICK LAYER ON A SHEET PAN. FREEZE UNTIL MOUSSE IS SET, ABOUT ONE HOUR.

6. USING A COOKIE CUTTER, CUT MOUSSE INTO A 3 1/2-INCH DISC.

7. GARNISH ON TOP WITH WHIPPED CREAM ROSETTES.

## MERINGUE POODLE (SWISS STYLE MERINGUE)

1. PREHEAT OVEN TO 200ºF.

2. DRAW AND CUT A HOLE IN THE BOARD IN THE SHAPE OF A SMALL FRENCH POODLE, ABOUT 3 1/2 INCHES IN LENGTH (FROM FRONT PAWS TO HIND PAWS).

3. ADD EGG WHITES, SUGAR AND FOOD COLORING IN A BOWL SET OVER A PAN OF SIMMERING WATER (A WATER BATH). STIR CONTINUOUSLY UNTIL THEY REACH 100ºF AND SUGAR IS COMPLETELY DISSOLVED. REMOVE BOWL FROM PAN OF WATER, AND WHIP EGG WHITES SO THAT THEY FORM SOFT PEAKS.

## HAZELNUT CRUNCH BASE

5 OZ. SEMI-SWEET CHOCOLATE

1 1/2 POUNDS PRALINOSA (HAZELNUT PASTE)

12 OZ. VANILLA WAFERS (CRUSHED)

## CHOCOLATE MOUSSE

21 OZ. SEMI-SWEET CHOCOLATE

1 QUART HEAVY CREAM

5 EGG YOLKS

5 EGG WHITES

4 OZ. GRANULATED SUGAR

## MERINGUE

8 OZ. EGG WHITES

1 POUND GRANULATED SUGAR

4 DROPS RED FOOD COLORING

## SPECIAL EQUIPMENT:

STYRO BOARD OR BAKING PAN LINER PAPER, CIRCULAR COOKIE CUTTERS

4. BUTTER AND FLOUR A LARGE BAKING SHEET. PLACE TEMPLATE ON SHEET. USING THE TEMPLATE
   AS A GUIDE, SPREAD THE MERINGUE INTO THE DESIRED SHAPE ON THE BAKING SHEET. REMOVE
   TEMPLATE.

5. BAKE IN OVEN FOR 1 HOUR AND 15 MINUTES (CHECK PROGRESS AFTER 45 MINUTES).

## TO ASSEMBLE

PLACE MOUSSE DISK ON HAZELNUT BASE. STAND MERINGUE POODLE VERTICALLY ON TOP OF
   MOUSSE DISK.

# Miss Celie's Bananas Foster
# avec Chocolat

**Olde Victorian Inn and Spa, New Orleans,** This is an old Creole recipe served by Miss Celie Brune in 1893 to her rooming house dinner guests (many of New Orleans prominent Madams and prostitutes). It is now served at the Olde Victorian Inn bed & breakfast and Miss Celie's day spa. The Olde Victorian Inn was awarded "Best Breakfast" from Frommers Travel Guide, which gives official confirmation of what everyone visiting New Orleans already knows. (Editors Note: Olde Victorian closed after Hurricane Katrina)

## Chocolate Sauce

1. Combine sugar and cocoa in a heavy sauce pan. Add whipping cream and stir. Bring to a slow boil stirring constantly. Reduce heat and cook until thick, stirring constantly.
2. Remove from heat and add vanilla extract.

## Bananas Foster

1. Melt butter and sugar in a sauce pan over medium heat. Cook for about 1 minute, allowing the sugar to slightly brown and caramelize.
2. Stir in cinnamon, lemon juice, maple syrup, rum and Kahlúa. Cook for 2 minutes to allow alcohol to evaporate a bit. Be careful to remove pan briefly from flame when adding the alcohol.
3. Add bananas, baste in cinnamon sauce, and simmer until warm.

## To Serve

1. Dip the rims of champagne glasses (not flutes) into a bowl with the chocolate sauce, then dip in a bowl with the graham cracker crumbs.
2. Using a spoon, fill glass with the Bananas Foster.
3. Drizzle chocolate sauce over the top of the warm Bananas Foster. Serve at once. Serves 4

## Chocolate Sauce

1/2 cup brown sugar

2/3 cup cocoa

2/3 cup whipping cream

1 Tbs vanilla extract

1 cup graham cracker crumbs

## Bananas Foster

3 Tbs butter

1/4 cup brown sugar

1 cup maple syrup

1/8 tsp ground cinnamon

4 bananas sliced (not too ripe)

1 Tbs lemon juice

1/4 cup rum

2 Tbs Kahlúa (Coffee Liqueur)

# CHOCOLATE ESPRESSO SOUFFLÉ

**Broussard's Restaurant, Chef Gunter Preuss, New Orleans,** Light in consistency yet savory and full of flavor, Chef Preuss' unique soufflé introduced New Orleans to an entirely new combination of traditional ingredients.

1. PREHEAT THE OVEN TO 375ºF.

2. LIGHTLY BUTTER A 1 1/2 TO 2-QUART SOUFFLÉ MOLD, OR SIX INDIVIDUAL-SIZE SOUFFLÉ MOLDS. SET ASIDE.

3. IN A DOUBLE BOILER, OR A BOWL SET OVER A PAN OF SIMMERING WATER, MELT THE SEMI-SWEET CHOCOLATE AND WHISK IN THE DOUBLE-STRENGTH ESPRESSO.

4. MAKE THE MERINGUE BY WHIPPING THE EGG WHITES IN A BOWL WITH A PINCH OF SALT UNTIL THEY FORM SOFT PEAKS. SLOWLY ADD THE SUGAR, CONTINUING TO WHIP THE WHITES AS YOU GO. WHIP UNTIL THE SUGAR IS DISSOLVED.

5. TRANSFER THE CHOCOLATE-ESPRESSO MIXTURE TO A BOWL AND FOLD IN SEVERAL TABLESPOONFULS OF THE MERINGUE TO LIGHTEN IT. FOLD IN THE REMAINING MERINGUE A THIRD AT A TIME. DO NOT OVERWORK THE MIXTURE.

6. SPOON THE SOUFFLÉ MIXTURE INTO THE BUTTERED SOUFFLÉ MOLD OR MOLDS. PLACE THE MOLDS IN A PAN OF HOT WATER AND THE WHOLE PAN INTO THE PREHEATED OVEN. BAKE FOR 35-40 MINUTES, OR UNTIL THE SOUFFLÉ HAS RISEN AND BROWNED NICELY ON THE TOP. SERVES 6

6 LARGE EGG WHITES

9 OZ. SEMISWEET CHOCOLATE, IN PIECES OR GRATED

1 CUP SUGAR

1 1/2 CUPS DOUBLE-STRENGTH ESPRESSO

1 TBS BUTTER

PINCH SALT

BUTTER FOR MOLDS

# Chocolate Pava

**Broussard's Restaurant, Chef Gunter Preuss, New Orleans**

1. In a double boiler, or a bowl set over a pan of simmering water, gently melt the chocolate and butter with the sugar, stirring to mix until the chocolate and sugar are dissolved. Cool the mixture in refrigerator to about room temperature.

2. Beat the egg yolks to the ribbon stage (drips like ribbons from a wooden spoon), add to the chocolate, and mix well. Return mixture to the refrigerator.

3. When chocolate mixture has completely cooled, in a separate bowl beat the egg whites to the stiff-peak stage.

4. Fold the egg whites into the chocolate a third at a time. Refrigerate chocolate mixture for about 30 minutes, or until Pava is set.

Serve with a raspberry sauce and freshly whipped cream. Serves 6

- 4 oz. unsweetened chocolate
- 5 eggs (separated into whites and yolks)
- 1/2 cup fresh butter
- 6 Tbs sugar
- 1 1/2 cups freshly whipped cream
- 2 cups of raspberry sauce

# WHITE CHOCOLATE BREAD PUDDING WITH WHITE CHOCOLATE KAHLÚA SAUCE

**Louisiana School of Cooking, Chef Patrick Mould, Lafayette, Louisiana,**
There is an unwritten rule that Louisiana bread pudding is hard to beat. The biggest challenge of this recipe is trying not to eat the pudding before the sauce is done.

## BREAD PUDDING

1. PREHEAT OVEN TO 350ºF.
2. PLACE CUBED FRENCH BREAD IN LARGE CASSEROLE DISH AND TOAST BREAD FOR 15 MINUTES. REMOVE FROM OVEN.
3. PLACE HEAVY CREAM, MILK AND SUGAR IN A MEDIUM SAUCE PAN AND HEAT JUST UNTIL THE BOILING POINT. REMOVE FROM HEAT, ADD WHITE CHOCOLATE AND STIR UNTIL CHOCOLATE HAS MELTED.
4. IN A SEPARATE BOWL, WHIP TOGETHER WHOLE EGGS AND EGG YOLKS. ADD TO CREAM AND WHIP UNTIL INCORPORATED. POUR MIXTURE OVER TOASTED FRENCH BREAD AND ALLOW TO SOAK FOR 20 MINUTES. PLACE IN OVEN AND BAKE 35 MINUTES COVERED. UNCOVER AND BAKE FOR AN ADDITIONAL 15 MINUTES.

## KAHLÚA SAUCE

1. BRING HEAVY CREAM AND KAHLÚA TO A SIMMER IN A SMALL SAUCEPAN FOR 3-5 MINUTES. SERVES 12
2. REMOVE FROM HEAT AND ADD CHOCOLATE. ALLOW CREAM TO SIT, STIRRING OCCASIONALLY UNTIL CHOCOLATE IS MELTED. STIR UNTIL SMOOTH.

## TO SERVE

TOP EACH BREAD PUDDING SERVING WITH KAHLÚA SAUCE.

## BREAD PUDDING

**6 CUPS CUBED FRENCH BREAD
(APPROXIMATELY 2 LOAFS)**
**4 CUPS HEAVY CREAM**
**1 CUP MILK**
**1/2 CUP SUGAR**
**8 OZ. WHITE CHOCOLATE**
**2 WHOLE EGGS**
**5 EGG YOLKS**

## KAHLÚA SAUCE

**2 CUPS HEAVY CREAM**
**8 OZ. WHITE CHOCOLATE**
**1/4 CUP KAHLÚA
(COFFEE LIQUEUR)**

*If I may be tongue-in-cheek, the French have historically been ground-breaking in adventurous endeavors in regards to the tongue - consider the French kiss, the Marquis de Sade and the taste for chocolate.*

**- Jim Kastleman, Publisher**
**PaperCity Magazine**

*My grandmother prepared the original version of her specialty coffee, "Caffe D'Amore Con Un Baccio" in Bellagio Italy in 1923, using Belgian chocolate as the foundational ingredient in her beverage creation.*

**- Paul Comi, President**
**Caffe D'Amore Inc.**

*In Genesis 8 - 21, which describes the scene after the great flood, the Bible states; "And the Lord smelled a sweet savor; and the Lord said in his heart, I will not again curse the ground any more for man's sake." I'd like to think the sweet savor the Lord smelled was chocolate, and that chocolate has been soothing His wrath for the last 5,000 years. At least that's the rationalization I make when devouring a handful.*

**- Ronald Margulis**
**Food Writer, Art Critic**
**President of RAM Communications**

*Above: A jazz band in Nice, France*
*Opposite Page: Fouquet*

## JOAN OSBURN, FOUNDER OF CAFE SOCIETY, NAPA, CALIFORNIA, ON WHERE TO GO IN PARIS FOR CHOCOLAT CHAUD (HOT CHOCOLATE)

My rapturous love affair is with Angelina's chocolate chaud (en tasse) from Paris. Opened in 1903 as Rumpelmayer on 226 Rue de Rivoli and frequented by Marcel Proust and Coco Chanel, Angelina is still an elegant salon de thé. Not in the same category as ordinary hot chocolate, people stand in line for hours to savour this "chocolat Africain." While impossible to describe with words, I can best say that the experience is something akin to sipping the warm sweet nectar of an exquisite chocolate truffle. I find this to be the finest hot chocolate experience in the world.

**Angelina's**
*226, rue de Rivoli, Paris*

*The Louvre with Hot Chocolate, photograph courtesy of Karin Smith*

## CARA BLACK, AUTHOR OF *Murder in Clichy* AND *Murder in the Bastille*, ON WHERE TO GO IN PARIS FOR CHOCOLAT CHAUD (HOT CHOCOLATE)

True French chocolate at Laduree -- the monstrously rich, are-you-kidding-me, served-with-a-side-of-whipped cream kind. So thick your spoon stands up in it. And with the fancy tea room ambiance of Paris.

As a child (Vincent), once a year at Christmas, his mother would take him for lunch with "a gentleman friend. Always at posh Laduree, famous for thick hot chocoate, in Place de la Madeleine...Vincent would thank him and spoon up the hot chocolate. "Growing a mustache?" the man would joke about the chocolate swipe on Vincent's upper lip.

Text from *Murder in the Bastille*

*Ladurée*
422, rue Saint Honoré
at Place de la Madeleine

## DIANA BARRAND, OWNER OF LE ZINC FRENCH BISTRO, SAN FRANCISCO, ON WHERE TO GO IN PARIS FOR CHOCOLATE

My favorite place is:

### Berthillon
*31, rue Saint-Louis-en-l'Ile*
This family run ice-cream maker is the most famous in Paris. Long lines are seen coming out the door of the original ice cream shop on the Ile Saint Louis. The ice creams are also now found in select Parisian cafes. The most decadent and remarkable in my opinion is the chocolate ice cream. It is so rich in chocolate that it has to be kept in the fridge rather than the freezer.

Berthillon offers over 60 different flavors of glace (ice cream) and sorbet.

# CHOCOLAT CHAUD WITH CREAMY MELTED BARS OF DARK CHOCOLATE

**Caroline Isautier-Rougeot, Frenchparents.net,** "In France a truly good cocoa ( with no added sugar) in powdered form is the Van Houtten brand ( i.e Dutch cocoa). In the U.S., Peet's Coffee & Tea makes a delicious cocoa powder as well. In addition, you can buy the Angelina brand hot cocoa mix at various places. Angelina is a 'salon de thé' in Paris that makes the richest and thickest chocolat chaud ever, mostly because it tastes just like pure melted chocolate bars." Caroline demonstrates this concept with the following recipe.

1. FINELY SLICE THE CHOCOLATE BAR WITH A SERRATED BREAD KNIFE.

2. STIR TOGETHER THE MILK, WATER AND SUGAR IN A SAUCEPAN. BRING TO A BOIL OVER MEDIUM HEAT. ADD THE CHOPPED CHOCOLATE AND THE COCOA AND BRING TO A BOIL AGAIN, WHISKING UNTIL THE CHOCOLATE AND THE COCOA ARE DISSOLVED AND THE MIXTURE HAS THICKENED. REDUCE THE HEAT TO VERY LOW.

3. BLEND FOR 5 MINUTES WITH A STICK BLENDER OR IN A BLENDER FOR 30 SECONDS, UNTIL THICK AND FOAMY.

4. BLEND FOR 5 MINUTES WITH A STICK BLENDER OR IN A BLENDER FOR 30 SECONDS, UNTIL THICK AND FOAMY.

2 1/4 CUPS WHOLE MILK

1/4 CUP WATER

1/4 CUP SUPERFINE GRANU-LATED SUGAR

ONE 3.5 OZ. BAR OF SCHARFFEN BERGER, VALRHONA OR LINDT BITTER-SWEET DARK CHOCOLATE

1/4 CUP COCOA POWDER, PREF-ERABLY VALRHONA

# CHOCOLATE FRENCH TOAST

## PAIN PERDU AU CHOCOLAT

Pain perdu translates literally as "lost bread," which is what it would be if not for this kind of recipe. The key to good pain perdu is not to take it too seriously. After all, it's just day-old bread that has been revitalized through the magic of chemistry and cuisine. Of course, because it was the French who promoted this technique, not only do they have it named after them, but they get to think of creative new ways to prepare it.

1. SLOWLY HEAT MILK IN A SAUCEPAN, THEN ADD CHOCOLATE TO THE WARM MILK TO MELT, STIRRING FREQUENTLY. REMOVE FROM HEAT WHEN CHOCOLATE HAS MELTED.

2. IN A BOWL, COMBINE THE CHOCOLATE MILK, ALL THE SPICES, AND THE EGGS.

3. WHISK UNTIL EGGS ARE THOROUGHLY INTEGRATED.

4. ADD BREAD PIECES TO BOWL, PUSHING DOWN SO THAT EACH PIECE IS COMPLETELY SOAKED.

5. BUTTER AND HEAT A FRYING PAN (MEDIUM-HIGH HEAT). ADD BREAD PIECES AND COOK UNTIL LIGHT TO MEDIUM-BROWN ON EACH SIDE. PRESS DOWN WITH SPATULA TO ENSURE THOROUGH COOKING OF THE INSIDE OF THE BREAD (BREAD SHOULD NOT BE SOGGY ONCE COOKED). SERVES 4-8. SERVE WITH BUTTER OR JAM

2 CUPS OF MILK

3 EGGS

1 TBS OF GROUND CINNAMON

2 TSP OF GROUND NUTMEG

1 TSP OF VANILLA EXTRACT

1 1/2 OZ. OF SEMI-SWEET CHOCOLATE, CHOPPED (SCHARFFEN BERGER OR E. GUITTARD)

8 PIECES OF 1-2 INCH SLICES OF DAY OLD BAGUETTE, OR PIECES OF REGULAR SLICED WHITE, SOURDOUGH OR WHEAT BREAD

BUTTER FOR COOKING

*Empress Joséphine, wife of Napoléan*

*....research continues on whether she favored pain perdu ou non. Most of this research takes place during breakfast time.*

# PEAR AND CHOCOLATE TART

**Lycée Français La Perouse, Anne De Kouchkovsky, the International French School, San Francisco**

1. CUT BUTTER INTO SMALL PIECES. IN A BOWL, USE AN ELECTRIC MIXER TO BLEND FLOUR, SUGAR AND BUTTER. MIX FOR 30 SECONDS. ADD EGG. MIX AGAIN UNTIL THE DOUGH BEGINS TO HOLD TOGETHER. CHILL DOUGH AT LEAST ONE HOUR IN REFRIGERATOR.

2. PREHEAT OVEN TO 450ºF.

3. TAKE DOUGH OUT OF REFRIGERATOR AND ALLOW TO WARM FOR 15 MINUTES. ROLL THE DOUGH INTO A CIRCLE USING A ROLLING PIN, AND PLACE IN AN 11-INCH TART PAN. TRIM EXCESS DOUGH FROM EDGES. USING A FORK, POKE SMALL HOLES IN THE DOUGH AT THE BOTTOM OF THE PAN. PLACE IN OVEN FOR 10 MINUTES.

4. IN A BOWL, USE AN ELECTRIC MIXER TO PURÉE PEARS (DRAIN SYRUP FIRST IF USING CANNED PEARS).

5. ADD THE FLOUR, CRÈME FRAÎCHE, SUGAR AND EGGS TO PEAR PURÉE. MIX ONCE AGAIN.

6. WHEN FILLING IS COMPLETELY BLENDED, POUR INTO THE TART PAN. COOK IN OVEN FOR 25 MINUTES.

7. PLACE COOKED TART IN REFRIGERATOR TO CHILL.

8. IN A PYREX GLASS OR OTHER MICROWAVE-SAFE BOWL, CUT THE CHOCOLATE INTO SMALL PIECES AND MELT PER PAGE 28. LET COOL SLIGHTLY.

9. SPREAD MELTED CHOCOLATE CAREFULLY ONTO CHILLED TART, ALLOW TO SIT AT LEAST FIVE MINUTES, THEN SERVE.

## FILLING

5 LARGE PEARS, PEELED AND CORED, OR A 25 OZ. CAN OF PEARS IN SYRUP

3 EGGS

1 TBS ALL PURPOSE FLOUR

1/3 CUP AND 1 TBS CRÈME FRAÎCHE

1/3 CUP AND 1 TBS GRANU-LATED SUGAR

2 TBS PEAR LIQUEUR (OPTIONAL)

5.25 OZ. DARK CHOCOLATE FOR ICING (FOR EXAMPLE, LINDT 70%)

## PÂTE SABLÉE / TART DOUGH

2 CUPS FLOUR

12 TBS BUTTER, SLIGHTLY SOFTENED

1/2 CUP GRANULATED SUGAR

1 EGG

# PETITS POTS AU CHOCOLAT

**Le Cordon Bleu, Paris,** These dainty little chocolate custards are prepared and cooked in a very similar way to crème caramel, except that they are much richer, with a fine, smooth melt-in-the-mouth texture. They must be allowed to cool completely before serving.

1. PREHEAT THE OVEN TO 325ºF.

2. PLACE THE MILK, CREAM, CHOCOLATE AND VANILLA BEAN IN A HEAVY-BOTTOMED SAUCEPAN AND BRING GENTLY TO A BOIL.

3. PUT THE EGG, EGG YOLKS AND SUGAR INTO A BOWL AND WHISK UNTIL CREAMY AND LIGHT.

4. POUR IN THE HOT CHOCOLATE MIXTURE AND STIR WITH A WOODEN SPOON TO BLEND. STRAIN INTO A LARGE LIQUID MEASURING CUP AND REMOVE THE VANILLA BEAN. SKIM ANY FROTH FROM THE TOP OF THE MIXTURE USING A METAL SPOON.

5. POUR THE MIXTURE INTO 6 X 1/3-CUP CERAMIC POTS OR ESPRESSO CUPS, FILLING THEM TO THE TOP. SET THE POTS IN A BAKING DISH AND POUR IN ENOUGH HOT WATER TO COME UP TO ABOUT 1/2 BELOW THEIR RIMS. (IN FRENCH CULINARY TERMS THIS IS KNOWN AS A "BAIN-MARIE" OR WATER-BATH.) BAKE FOR 30 MINUTES, OR UNTIL THE SURFACE OF THE CUSTARD FEELS ELASTIC WHEN TOUCHED AND YOUR FINGER PULLS AWAY CLEAN. IF NOT, CONTINUE COOKING A LITTLE LONGER.

6. REMOVE THE POTS FROM THE BAIN-MARIE AND SET ASIDE TO COOL.

7. FIT A PASTRY BAG WITH A STAR-SHAPED NOZZLE AND FILL WITH WHIPPED CREAM. PIPE ROSETTES OF CREAM ON THE TOP OF THE COOLED CHOCOLATE POTS AND SPRINKLE WITH GRATED CHOCOLATE. SERVES 6

1 1/2 CUPS MILK

1/3 CUP WHIPPING CREAM

2 OZ. SEMISWEET CHOCOLATE, CHOPPED

1/2 VANILLA BEAN, SPLIT LENGTHWISE

1 EGG

3 EGG YOLKS

1/3 CUP SUGAR

WHIPPED CREAM AND GRATED CHOCOLATE, TO SERVE

## PAULE CAILLAT, OF PROMENADES GOURMANDES, ON APPRECIATING AND DISCOVERING CHOCOLATE

I think we love chocolate in France because it is so delicious, and can take many different forms. We have a long history with it, but more importantly we treat chocolate as we do everything else - with refinement and minimalism. We do not exaggerate our consumption. Chocolate is considered as one of many pleasures, to be had in reasonable quantities.

In Paris, I give hands-on cooking classes, market tours and gourmet tours in English, mostly to Americans. I customize my menus to please their tastes, and always give a choice of desserts: fruit or chocolate. Chocolate is chosen 75% of the time. Of course, to me chocolate must maintain its original cocoa butter content, otherwise it is not worthy of being called chocolate. Since I have been using Valrhona, I am in heaven. For the moment, I use a variety (cru in French, referring to the beans) called Manjari, 64% cocoa content. Having such a good quality ingredient does practically all the work. For instance, in the *tarte au chocolat* that I make regularly in my cooking class, I prepare a Joel Robuchon ganache with equal weights of Valrhona and heavy cream, and use just one egg for the binding. It has no sugar at all, and is the only tarte au chocolat recipe I have ever found which calls for only one egg (others have a minimum of 3).

My mother's family comes from Brussels, and I love the Belgian "pralines" (which describes chocolate candies of varied shapes and fillings). My favorites are filled with either crème fraîche or pâte d'amande, a very personal taste. The best brands are Neuhaus, Corne de la Toison d'Or and Wittamer. Wittamer is actually a patisserie with no branch stores, so its pralines are available only in Brussels. Bernachon, the famous patisserie and chocolatier confiseur in Lyon, is a bit like Wittamer with no stores anywhere else, and in my opinion is the best in France.

My latest discovery is in Lausanne, Switzerland, where I found a very old-fashioned shop that sells "*chocolat au marteau*" (hammered chocolate). These are very large plaques of chocolate, not very thick, mostly dark chocolate, and mixed with either a nut or a dried fruit. The surface is uneven, as if the chocolate had actually been hammered. There must be at least 30 different flavors available. I had to wait in line for about 30 minutes, because the place is narrow, and when my turn came I ordered many different flavors. Each time I ordered the saleslady broke off a piece and weighed it on a very old-fashioned scale. It took at least 30 more minutes to complete my purchase. The clients behind me were complaining, but the shop lady, very elegant and efficient, told them to keep quiet. The entire experience was unique, and the chocolates delicious. From what I remember, it is a very old method of chocolate fabrication, probably the only place where it is still done.

# Crème Brûlée au chocolat

## Paule Caillat, Promenades Gourmandes, Paris

8 OZ. SEMISWEET CHOCOLATE (VALRHONA OR SCHARFFEN BERGER)

1 1/2 CUPS HEAVY CREAM

3/4 CUP MILK

7 EGG YOLKS

1/2 CUP GRANULATED SUGAR

6 TBS ICING SUGAR, OR RAW SUGAR

SPECIAL EQUIPMENT:
6 RAMEKINS

1. BREAK THE CHOCOLATE INTO SMALL PIECES AND SET ASIDE IN A BOWL.
2. BRING THE MILK AND CREAM TO A BOIL TOGETHER IN A SAUCEPAN.
3. IN A SEPARATE BOWL, WHISK THE EGG YOLKS WITH THE SUGAR UNTIL THOROUGHLY BLENDED (THE EGG YOLKS WILL BE PALE AND CREAMY).
4. POUR THE HOT CREAM/MILK MIXTURE OVER THE YOLKS, WHISKING TO BLEND, THEN RETURN TO LOW HEAT IN THE SAUCEPAN AND COOK, STIRRING CONSTANTLY, UNTIL THE MIXTURE THICKENS AND COATS THE BACK OF A WOODEN SPOON. DO NOT LET THIS CUSTARD MIXTURE BOIL.
5. WHILE STILL HOT, POUR HALF OF THE CUSTARD MIXTURE OVER THE CHOCOLATE. WHISK UNTIL SMOOTH, AND REPEAT WITH THE REMAINING HALF, STIRRING TO MAKE SURE IT IS SMOOTH.
6. FILL THE RAMEKINS WITH THE CUSTARD MIXTURE AND REFRIGERATE UNTIL SET (APPROXIMATELY 2 HOURS).
7. REMOVE FROM REFRIGERATOR. FIFTEEN MINUTES BEFORE SERVING, PREHEAT THE OVEN BROILER, THEN SPRINKLE THE TOP OF EACH CRÈME BRULEE WITH ONE TABLESPOON OF SUGAR. PLACE ON THE TOP RACK OF THE OVEN BENEATH THE BROILER, AND ALLOW THE SUGAR TO TURN BROWN AND CARAMELIZE FOR

APPROXIMATELY 2 TO 3 MINUTES. YOU CAN ALSO CARAMELIZE THE SUGAR USING A KITCHEN/PASTRY BLOW TORCH. WHEN COMPLETED, ALLOW CARAMEL TO COOL BEFORE SERVING. SERVES 6. USUALLY SERVED CHILLED.

# PÂTE À CHOUX

## CREAM PUFF DOUGH

### Paule Caillat, Promenades Gourmandes, Paris

1. PLACE THE BUTTER IN A SAUCEPAN WITH THE WATER, MILK, SUGAR AND SALT. STIR, THEN BRING SLOWLY TO A BOIL, ALLOWING THE BUTTER TO MELT.

2. AS SOON AS THE BUTTER IS MELTED, REMOVE THE SAUCEPAN FROM HEAT. ADD ALL THE FLOUR INTO THE LIQUID AT ONCE, THEN MIX WITH A WOODEN SPOON UNTIL SMOOTH.

3. RETURN TO HEAT AND CONTINUE TO STIR. REMOVE FROM HEAT WHEN DOUGH NO LONGER STICKS TO THE SIDES OF THE POT. TRANSFER TO A BOWL AND LET MIXTURE COOL SLIGHTLY.

4. ADD THE EGGS ONE AT A TIME, MIXING EACH THOROUGH-LY UNTIL TOTALLY ABSORBED INTO THE DOUGH. THE CHOUX DOUGH SHOULD BE SMOOTH, SHINY AND THICK. STIR IT A BIT MORE WITH THE SPATULA TO ADD AIR TO THE DOUGH AND TO LIGHTEN ITS TEXTURE.

5. SET THE CHOUX DOUGH ASIDE FOR USE IN PROFITER-OLES, ÉCLAIRS, OR CREAM PUFFS.

FOR APPROXIMATELY 20 LARGE CHOUX

1 CUP FLOUR, ALL-PURPOSE
8 TBS UNSALTED BUTTER
1/2 CUP WATER
1/2 CUP MILK
5 EGGS
1 TBS GRANULATED SUGAR
1/2 TSP SALT

# PROFITEROLES

## Paule Caillat, Promenades Gourmandes, Paris

### PASTRY PUFFS

1. PREHEAT THE OVEN TO 375ºF.

2. BUTTER A BAKING SHEET (OR USE A NON-STICK BAKING SHEET).

3. USING EITHER A PASTRY BAG OR TWO SPOONS (ONE TO SCOOP THE DOUGH AND THE OTHER TO PUSH IT OFF THE FIRST SPOON), MAKE PUFF-SIZED BALLS OF PÂTE DOUGH AND PLACE THEM ON THE SHEET. MAKE SURE THEY ARE FAR ENOUGH APART THAT THEY DO NOT TOUCH WHEN THEY EXPAND DURING BAKING.

4. IN A BOWL, BEAT THE EGG AND SALT. TO FORM A GLAZE, BRUSH THE TOP OF EACH PUFF WITH THE EGG, THEN INDENT THE TOP OF EACH PUFF WITH THE BACK OF A FORK DIPPED IN THE EGG.

5. BAKE FOR 25 MINUTES. DO NOT OPEN THE OVEN DOOR FOR THE FIRST 15 MINUTES OF BAKING, THEN KEEP DOOR AJAR FOR THE REMAINING 10 MINUTES.

6. VERIFY THAT THE CHOUX IS COOKED BEFORE TAKING OUT OF OVEN. THE PASTRY PUFFS SHOULD BE GOLDEN BROWN AND THE BASES SHOULD BE YELLOW. REMOVE AND ALLOW TO COOL.

### CHOCOLATE SAUCE

1. ADD CHOCOLATE AND WATER INTO A POT. HEAT SLOWLY, STIRRING WITH A WHISK UNTIL CHOCOLATE IS MELTED. REMOVE FROM HEAT.

2. ADD THE BUTTER, ALLOW TO MELT, THEN STIR WELL FOR A VERY SMOOTH TEXTURE.

### TO ASSEMBLE

1. CUT EACH PUFF HORIZONTALLY IN TWO ACROSS THE BASE AND FILL WITH A SCOOP OF VANILLA ICE-CREAM OR WHIPPED CREAM. PLACE THE UPPER-HALF OF EACH PUFF BACK ON TOP OF THE CREAM.

### PASTRY PUFFS

PÂTE À CHOUX SUCRÉE (CREAM PUFF DOUGH), PER RECIPE ON PAGE 132

1 EGG FOR THE EGG WASH (A GLAZE)

A PINCH OF SALT

### FILLING

1 PINT OF VANILLA ICE-CREAM OR WHIPPED CREAM

### CHOCOLATE SAUCE

10 OZ. CHOCOLATE, CHOPPED (65% COCOA)

3 TBS WATER

3 1/2 TBS UNSALTED BUTTER, CUT INTO SMALL PIECES

2. POUR THE WARM CHOCOLATE SAUCE OVER PUFFS AND SERVE IMMEDIATELY.
SERVES 8

NOTES: IF MAKING CHOCOLATE SAUCE AHEAD OF TIME, KEEP WARM IN A BAIN-MARIE OR A BOWL OVER WARM WATER. ONCE YOU HAVE FILLED THE "CHOUX" WITH ICE-CREAM, KEEP THEM IN THE FREEZER IF YOU HAVE TO WAIT A WHILE BEFORE SERVING.

# ÉCLAIRS

"I find it difficult to disagree with the possibility that the height of luxury might not be an expensive car, a yacht in Monte Carlo, or a villa in Jamaica, but may instead be a really, really, really good chocolate éclair." - André K. Crump

## ÉCLAIR SHELLS

PÂTE À CHOUX SUCRÉE (CREAM PUFF DOUGH), PER RECIPE ON PAGE 132

1 EGG FOR THE EGG WASH (A GLAZE)

A PINCH OF SALT

## CRÈME PATISSIERE

6 EGG YOLKS

1/2 CUP SUGAR

6 TBS FLOUR

2 TBS CORNSTARCH

2 CUPS OF MILK

2 TSP OF VANILLA EXTRACT

WHIPPED CREAM CAN BE SUBSTITUTED FOR CRÈME PATISSIERE

## CHOCOLATE ICING

10 OZ. DARK CHOCOLATE, CHOPPED

3 TBS MILK

4 TBS UNSALTED BUTTER, CUT INTO SMALL PIECES

4 TBS SUGAR

## ÉCLAIR SHELLS

1. PREHEAT THE OVEN TO 400ºF.

2. BUTTER A BAKING SHEET (OR USE A NON-STICK BAKING SHEET).

3. USING A PASTRY BAG WITH A 1/2-INCH NOZZLE, PIPE 3 TO 4-INCH LONG LOGS OF PÂTE DOUGH ON THE SHEET. ALLOW ADEQUATE SPACING.

4. IN A BOWL, BEAT THE EGG AND SALT TO FORM A GLAZE. BRUSH THE TOP OF EACH LOG WITH THE EGG. USE A FORK DIPPED IN THE EGG GLAZE TO SCORE THE TOP OF THE LOG (WITH THE FORK FACING BACKWARDS, DRAW THE FORK DOWN THE LENGTH OF THE LOG TO MAKE A ROW OF SHALLOW LINES).

5. BAKE FOR 25-30 MINUTES, UNTIL LIGHT GOLDEN BROWN AND SOMEWHAT CRISP, BUT NOT HARD. REMOVE FROM OVEN AND COOL ON A WIRE RACK.

## CHOCOLATE ICING

SLOWLY BRING BUTTER, SUGAR AND MILK TO A LOW BOIL IN A SAUCEPAN, STIRRING TO MAKE SURE SUGAR DISSOLVES. ADD CHOCOLATE AND REMOVE FROM HEAT. STIR UNTIL CHOCOLATE HAS MELTED AND ICING IS A SMOOTH TEXTURE. ALLOW TO COOL A BIT BEFORE USING.

## CRÈME PATISSIERE

1. IN A BOWL, WHISK EGGS AND SUGAR TOGETHER UNTIL THEY THICKEN AND ARE PALE YELLOW. FOLD IN THE FLOUR AND CORNSTARCH.

2. IN A SAUCEPAN, BRING THE MILK TO A LOW BOIL, THEN POUR HOT MILK INTO THE BOWL OF EGG YOLKS. STIR WELL, THEN POUR MIXTURE BACK INTO SAUCEPAN AND HEAT TO A BOIL. LOWER HEAT AND ALLOW CRÈME TO THICKEN, STIRRING REGULARLY. WHEN THICKENED, REMOVE PAN FROM HEAT, POUR INTO A BOWL AND MIX IN VANILLA EXTRACT. COVER THE CRÈME WITH PARCHMENT PAPER OR WRAPPING PAPER, WHICH PREVENTS A SKIN FROM FORMING ON TOP, AND CHILL TO COOL.

## TO ASSEMBLE

MAKE A HORIZONTAL SLICE DOWN THE LENGTH OF EACH ÉCLAIR SHELL. PIPE OR SPOON CRÈME PATISSIERE (OR WHIPPED CREAM) INTO THE CAVITY OF THE ÉCLAIR SHELL. IF REMOVED, PLACE THE UPPER-HALF OF EACH ÉCLAIR BACK ON TOP OF THE CREAM. SPOON THE WARM CHOCOLATE ICING ON THE TOP OF THE ÉCLAIR, OR DIP THE ÉCLAIR INTO THE ICING.

## Dans les pharmacies
Charles Trenet

*[excerpt]*

Dans les pharmacies,
Dans les pharmacies...

On veut du nougat et du chocolat,
Des bonbons au citron, des stylos,
Des poupées gentilles
Pour les petites filles
Et, pour les garçons
Des lapins qui sont
Sauteurs et polissons.

*[translation]*

In the pharmacies,
In the pharmacies...

They sell nougat and chocolate,
Lemon candies, and pens,
Nice little dolls
For the little girls
And, for the boys
Rabbits who are
Jumpers and naughty.

Debauve & Gallais, Royal chocolatiers and
former pharmacists

# DEBAUVE & GALLAIS, PARIS

Debauve & Gallais is the godfather of Paris chocolatiers. Their motto is *"Appointed chocolate maker of the former Kings of France."* In France, where the citizens removed the actual head of the royal Head of State, that claim says a lot. It says that this chocolate has been good enough to endure revolutions, wars, and centuries. Founded in 1800 by Sulpice Debauve and his nephew Auguste Gallais, both former chemists, the shop was initially known for its chocolate-based pharmaceuticals. As the claimed medical benefits of chocolate were quite in vogue, the "fine and healthy chocolates" of Debauve & Gallais enjoyed a visible and notable business. Over time they were praised by writers, artists, aristocrats, gourmands, and renowned physicians & professors of medicine. Anatole France was particularly fond of them. As chocolatiers they also were officially approved by His Majesty Louis XVI, as well as by other monarchs, including Charles X and Louis-Phillipe.

The little shop with the half-moon counter at 30, rue de Saint Pères has been there since the early 1800's. It was designed by Percier & Fontaine, the very same architects who built La Malmaison for Empress Joséphine Bonaparte. In 1989 it was carefully restored, and has maintained much of its historical charm. There is also a more recent shop on 33, rue Vivienne, which also captures the Debauve & Gallais magic.

If you like your chocolate dark, this is the place to go. Their chocolates range from 60 to 72%, and even 85 to 99%, cocoa content, and contain no more than a modicum of sugar. Instead, these artisans rely on 'terroir, cru, and tradition,' along with fillings such as high quality pralines and ganache. Known not only for its chocolates and confections, but also for its boxes and luxurious presentation, Debauve & Gallais embodies many of the styles and practices that we now associate with the finest French chocolate establishments.

## CHOCOLATE IN FRENCH LITERATURE

### Le Petit Pierre (excerpt in French)
### Anatole France, 1919

La chocolaterie Debauve et Gallais a très bon air. Je ne sais si je rêve mais je crois y avoir vu des trumeaux avec des rénommées qui pouvaient aussi bien célébrer Arcole et Lodi que la crème de cacao et les chocolats pralinés. Les jeunes filles brunes ou blondes s'occupaient, les unes a recouvrir les tablettes de chocolat d'une mince feuille de metal clair comme l'argent, les autres à envelopper deux par deux ces mêmes tablettes dans du papier blanc à vignettes et à fermer ces enveloppes avec de la cire qu'elles chauffaient à la flamme d'une petite lampe en fer blanc. Quand Maman avait fait son emplette, la matrone qui presidait cette assemblée de vierges sages prenait dans une coupe de cristal placée à son cote une pastille de chocolat qu'elle m'offrait avec un sourire.

### [English translation]

The chocolate maker Debauve & Gallais appears lovely. I don't know if I am dreaming but I believe I saw some wall paintings that could very well have been a representation of Arcole and Lodi just as well as that of cream of cocoa and praline chocolate. The young women, blondes and brunettes, were busy, some wrapping chocolate bars with a thin sheet of metal resembling silver, others packaging the same wrapped bars two at a time in a white paper with vignettes, sealing these envelopes with a wax they heated with a small tin lamp. When mother was done shopping, the matron who presided over this assembly of well-behaved virgins reached into a crystal bowl at her side and offered me a chocolate pastille with a smile.

# CELEBRITIES OF FRENCH CHOCOLATE

## Jean-Paul Hévin

*Salon de thé & chocolat*

*231, rue Saint-Honoré, Paris*

One of the young Turks of French chocolateries, Jean-Paul Hévin has jewelry-like boutiques in Paris and Japan, where citizens love great chocolate and Hévin is a celebrity. Before opening his shops, he worked alongside French legend Joel Robuchon. In 1986 Hévin was awarded *Meilleur Ouvrier de France* (France's top craftsman). According to the *Guide des Croqueurs de Chocolat* (Chocolate Lovers' Guide), "the chocolates produced by that cocoa bean aficionado feature a bitterness so excellent that even the most finicky of purists will be won over. At the same time, adventurous types will be satisfied with the unexpected flavors." Voila.

## Hédiard

*21, place de la Madeleine, Paris*

Take a shopping bag, because while you're buying top-notch chocolate you will also want to add a tin of tea, a box of biscuits, a bottle of wine, and a few very fresh spices. Hediard is both a tourist and local destination in Paris, with good reason.

## Fauchon

*26, place de la Madeleine, Paris*

Everything at Fauchon looks so good that sometimes people just stare awestruck and mesmerized through the store windows. The Paris store is a landmark, and the New York City location is a good place "to lunch."

## Bernachon

*42, Cours Franklin Roosevelt, Lyon*

A family-affair with only one store, Bernachon is one of the few artisan chocolatiers to try, and succeed, in making chocolate from scratch. This means going from the beginning steps of bean selection, sorting, and roasting, all the way to producing incredible bars of ecstasy-inducing chocolate. The best of everything goes into these delicacies, including walnuts, armagnac, vanilla, and gold.

## Michel Chaudun

*149, rue de l'Université, Paris*

Charming and intoxicating, the gorgeous sculpted chocolates in Chaudun are made in the back of the store. Chaudun's fans are very loyal, and there is a hint that this may be attributed to their instant addiction to his creations.

## Marquise de Sévigné

*32, Place de la Madeleine, Paris*

Named after that famous proponent of chocolate, this boutique captures much of her sophistication and charm. A lovely blue exterior invites you to a shop with blond wood countertops and display cases filled with exquisite blue boxes of chocolate.

## Jacques Torres Chocolate

*66 Water Street*
*Brooklyn, New York*

The American dream in cacao; *un Français* comes to America, makes fantastic chocolates, opens a shop, get a television show, and calls himself Mr. Chocolate. If all the French were this successful in delivering quality French products in an American context, America would be in big trouble.

## A Few (But Not All) of the French Chocolatiers to Know

*A L'Etoile d'Or*, 30 *Rue Fontaine, Paris*

*Christian Constant*, 37, *rue d'Assas, Paris*

*La Fontaine au Chocolat*, 201, *rue Saint-Honoré*
*Paris*

*Ladurée*, 16, *rue Royale, Paris*

*Le Fleuriste du Chocolat*, 49, *avenue de la*
*Bourdonnais, Paris*

*Lenôtre*, 44, *rue d'Auteuil, Paris*

*Patisserie Kubler*, 29 *avenue des Vosges*
*Strasbourg*

*Pierre Hermé*, 72, *rue Bonaparte, Paris*

*Thierry Mulhaupt - Patisserie*, 18 *rue du Vieux*
*Marché aux Poissons, Strasbourg*

# PÂTE BRISÉE

This is the shortcrust pastry dough which is used as the basis for so many apple, chocolate, and pear tarts. Some pâte brisées include eggs, salt, and different measurements for butter and flour. Depending on the combination the resulting crust will vary in flakiness, richness, thickness, or taste. We prefer the recipe below because it produces good, dependable results, and it is very easy to make and remember.

1. SIFT FLOUR INTO BOWL. SLICE BUTTER INTO CUBES, AND ADD INTO BOWL.

2. USING HANDS AND FINGERS, KNEED THE BUTTER INTO THE FLOUR UNTIL IT BEGINS TO MAKE A CRUMBLY DOUGH. IF YOU PREFER, A BLENDER CAN BE USED ON THE LOWEST SETTING.

3. ADD 2 TABLESPOONS COLD WATER, THEN KNEED DOUGH UNTIL THE WATER HAS FULLY MOISTENED THE ENTIRE AMOUNT . ADD 1 TABLESPOON COLD WATER, AND REPEAT.

4. WHEN DOUGH HAS BEGUN TO STICK TOGETHER, AND ACTUALLY REMOVES MOST OF THE DOUGH FROM YOUR FINGERS BACK INTO THE MASS, SHAPE DOUGH INTO A BALL. BE SURE NOT TO OVERWORK THE DOUGH OR THE CRUST WILL BE TOUGH IN TEXTURE.

5. LEAVE BALL IN BOWL, COVER BOWL, PLACE IN REFRIGERATOR FOR 1 HOUR.

6. WHEN READY TO USE THE PÂTE BRISÉE, REMOVE FROM REFRIGERATOR AND USE A ROLLING PIN TO FLATTEN INTO A CIRCULAR SHAPE LARGE ENOUGH TO FIT INTO A TART PAN.

**1 CUP FLOUR**

**8 TBS BUTTER, LIGHTLY SALTED OR UNSALTED, COLD OR COOL**

**3 TBS COLD WATER**

# FRENCH ACCENT MARKS

## Accent aigu with the letter e

é   Example: *thé, sauté, café, André, Joséphine*

## Accent grave with the letter e

è   Example: *crème, chocolatière*

## Accent grave with other letters

à, ù      Example: *à la mode, là, où*

Usage: Helps to distinguish words that look the same but have different meanings and context.

Example: *la* (the), *ou* (or), versus *là* (there), *où* (where)

## Accent circonflexe with the letter e

ê   Example: *pêche* (peach, or fishing), *même* (same, even)

Pronounced the same as è

## Accent circonflexe with other letters

â, û, î   Example: *goûter* (to taste), *gâteau, pâte, dîner*

## Tréma

ë, ï Example: *naïf* (naive, artless)

Usage: Helps to demonstrate that the vowel with the tréma should be pronounced distinctly and independently from the connecting vowels.

Example: na-if (na-eef)

# ADVERBS OF QUANTITY

Many adverbs that are related to expressions of quantity are followed by "de" or "d' " before the noun in reference. The articles, "le, la, les" are usually not included.

| | |
|---|---|
| **assez** | enough |
| **autant** | as much, as many |
| **beaucoup** | many, much, a lot |
| **combien** | how many, how much |
| **moins** | less, fewer (in math it means "minus") |
| **peu** | little, few |
| **plus** | more |
| **tant** | so much, many |
| **trop** | too many, too much |

Example:

Je ne peux pas manger **assez de** chocolat.

(I cannot eat enough chocolate)

Je ne peux pas boire **trop de** chocolat chaud, ce n'est pas possible.

(I cannot drink too much hot chocolate, it's not possible)

Vous avez acheté **combien de** gateaux au chocolat? Ils sont pour moi, n'est-ce pas?

(You bought how many chocolate cakes? They're for me then, isn't that so?)

# CHOCOSSISSON - CHOCOLATE SAUSAGE

**Lycée Français La Perouse, Anne De Kouchkovsky, the International French School, San Francisco,** Parent-chef Anne De Kouchkovsky teaches elementary students in the after-school cooking class at the Lycée Francais La Perouse, the International French School. Kids really love making this treat, and parents really love to sample their homework.

1. IN A BOWL, BEAT THE EGG YOLKS AND SUGAR UNTIL THE MIXTURE IS LIGHT IN COLOR.
2. MELT THE BUTTER IN A SAUCEPAN OR IN THE MICROWAVE, ADD TO THE SUGAR/EGG MIXTURE, THEN ADD THE COCOA. MIX WELL.
3. CRUMBLE THE COOKIES AND ADD THEM TO THE BATTER. STIR WELL TO FORM A DOUGH.
4. POUR THE DOUGH ONTO A SHEET OF ALUMINUM FOIL, THEN ROLL FOIL SO THAT IT MAKES THE DOUGH INTO THE FORM OF A SAUSAGE.
5. CHILL IN THE REFRIGERATOR FOR 3 TO 4 HOURS.
6. TAKE OFF THE ALUMINUM FOIL, ROLL IN POWDERED SUGAR, SLICE TO SERVE.

2/3 CUP BROWN SUGAR OR 1/2 CUP WHITE SUGAR

1 1/4 CUPS UNSWEETENED COCOA

9 TBS BUTTER

4 EGG YOLKS

20 PETITS-BEURRE COOKIES OR GRAHAM CRACKERS

POWDERED SUGAR FOR DUSTING

## ZIZI JEANMARIE

Actress and singer Zizi Jeanmaire was well known for her song, "La croqueuse de diamants" (The muncher of diamonds). A former prima ballerina of Les Ballets des Champs Elysee's, during the 1950s she performed in several film musicals in America and France. In French newspaper Le Monde, Dominique Fretard described her as "a head of black hair, face pale, with long legs that climbed all the way up to her thighs." After her film career ended, Zizi continued to perform, and was even known to sing a few songs of the talented renegade, Serge Gainsbourg. In "La croqueuse de diamants," rather than munch on chocolate or other energizing and savory delights, Zizi says she prefers to bite into something a bit crunchier.

We find it interesting that chocolate and diamonds are nonetheless so closely compared as the French breakfast of champions.

*La croqueuse de diamants*
Zizi Jeanmaire
**Paroles: Raymond Queneau. Musique: Men Michel Damase, Roland Petit**
**1950, (C) 1950 Editions Mondia S.A.**

### *[excerpt]*

Je suis une croqueuse de diamants
Oui le diamant c'est ma nourriture
Il convient à ma nature
J'aime quand ça m'criss' sous la dent
Des qu'ça brill' j'suis hors de moi
J'hesit' pas un seul instant
Et je bondis sur ma proie
Je suis un' croqueus' de diamants

La plus costaud' des athletes
Qu'a gagné tous les concours
La championn' de bicyclette
Qu'est la vainqueus' des Six Jours
Si ell's voulaient m'fair' confiance
Tripleraient leurs performances
Supprimer l'chocolat
Le matin avaler trois carats
Bien à jeun
Je suis une croqueuse de diamants

*[translation]*

I am the muncher of diamonds
Yes, diamonds are my food
It suits my nature
I love when they crunch under my teeth
When they shine I am beside myself
I only hesitate an instant
And I leap on my prey
I am the muncher of diamonds

The strongest athlete
Who has won all the competitions
The bicycle champion
Who is the winner of the "Six Jours"
If they want to trust me
And triple their performances
Do away with the chocolate
And swallow three carats in the morning
Better on an empty stomach
I am the muncher of diamonds

# PIEDMONTESE TRUFFLES

**Patisserie Kubler, Chef Antoine Hepp, Strasbourg,** Chef Hepp is the patriarch and manager of one of Strasbourg's most celebrated confectioneries. In addition to his local fame, he also has won the French national competition for "Meilleur Ouvrier de France" (Best Craftsman in France). Because of his reputation, Chef Hepp has had many students come from around the world to learn pastry-making, and has taught over 2000 pupils. According to him, "Chocolate is present in French palates since our early childhood, and it accompanies us throughout our entire existence. Chocolate is part of our gustative imagination, and we love it all the more because its bitterness makes our own disappear."

1. MELT CHOCOLATE FOR TRUFFLE. REMOVE FROM HEAT.

2. IN A SAUCEPAN, BRING THE CREAM TO A BOIL AND POUR IT ON THE MELTED CHOCOLATE, STIRRING FIRMLY.

3. STIR IN SUGAR AND SOFTENED BUTTER.

4. PLACE MIXTURE IN REFRIGERATOR FOR TWO HOURS.

5. REMOVE FROM REFRIGERATOR. USE A SPOON TO SCOOP OUT AMOUNTS OF THE CHOCOLATE TRUFFLE MIXTURE, AND USE YOUR HANDS TO SHAPE INTO BALLS. OR, YOU CAN ROLL IT ON A FLAT SURFACE TO GET SMALL BALLS. BEFORE YOU FINISH EACH TRUFFLE BALL, INSERT INSIDE ONE ROASTED HAZELNUT.

6. PLACE IN REFRIGERATOR.

7. MELT THE COUVERTURE MILK CHOCOLATE. LET COOL. (IF WANT YOU CAN TEMPER THE CHOCOLATE. ALLOW TO COOL UNTIL IT BECOMES SOLID, THEN SLOWLY REHEAT UNTIL IT MELTS AGAIN)

8. IN GROUPS OF 4 TO 5 BALLS, DIP THE TRUFFLES IN THE WARM (BUT NOT HOT) MELTED MILK CHOCOLATE COUVERTURE. TAKE OUT AND ROLL THE TRUFFLES IN CHOCOLATE SHAVINGS. SET TRUFFLES ASIDE TO COOL ON PARCHMENT PAPER OR NON-STICK COOKIE SHEET.

## TRUFFLE

14 OZ. MILK CHOCOLATE

3/4 CUP HEAVY CREAM

1 1/2 TBS BUTTER

1/4 CUP SUGAR

1/3 CUP OF WHOLE HAZELNUTS, ROASTED

## COATING

7 OZ. MILK CHOCOLATE COU-

VERTURE

3.5 OZ. MILK CHOCOLATE SHAVINGS

*An Alsatian-style brasserie in Paris*

# Swiss Dreams

## COCOA-COVERED, PRALINE-FILLED CHOCOLATES

**Chefs John Lehmann and Conny Züger, Switzerland**,
John Lehmann is a professor at the school of baking, pastry, confections and chocolates, in the Gruyere region of Switzerland. He holds the highest degree one can have in the country for these particular specialties. With this recipe, the "Swiss Dreams," John teams up with chocolate professional Conny Zuger to show how a few basic ingredients can make a fabulous Swiss-French confection.

1. ADD THE WATER, SUGAR AND VANILLA IN A SAUCEPAN, AND COOK OVER MEDIUM HEAT UNTIL THE SUGAR DISSOLVES, MAKING A SYRUP. USE TONGS OR A SPOON TO REMOVE THE VANILLA BEAN.

2. ADD THE ROASTED HAZELNUTS TO THE SUGAR, WATER AND VANILLA SYRUP AND STIR. THE SUGAR WILL BEGIN TO CRYSTALLIZE. CONTINUE TO STIR OVER MEDIUM HEAT UNTIL THE SUGAR CARAMELIZES. REMOVE FROM HEAT.

3. POUR CARAMELIZED HAZELNUTS ON A TABLE. (DO NOT TOUCH EITHER HOT CARAMEL OR CARAMELIZED HAZELNUTS WITH YOUR HANDS) PUT 2/3 OF THE WARM CARAMELIZED HAZELNUTS IMMEDIATELY INTO A BLENDER OR FOOD PROCESSOR, AND PUREE UNTIL IT MAKES A PRALINE PASTE.

4. COARSELY CHOP THE REMAINING 1/3 CARAMELIZED HAZELNUTS AND STIR INTO THE PRALINE PASTE. PLACE IN REFRIGERATOR TO COOL.

5. MELT THE CHOCOLATE. REMOVE FROM HEAT.

6. ADD MELTED CHOCOLATE TO THE PRALINE, AND STIR UNTIL THE MIXTURE BEGINS TO GET A BIT FIRM. USE A SPOON TO SCOOP OUT PORTIONS, AND PLACE EACH PORTION ON A NON-STICK BAKING SHEET OR PARCHMENT PAPER. THE DESIRED FORM CAN BE A BALL OR AN IRREGULAR SPHERE.

7. PLACE IN REFRIGERATOR AND ALLOW TO COOL AND HARDEN.

8. REMOVE FROM REFRIGERATOR AND ROLL IN THE CHOCOLATE POWDER OR IN SEMI-SWEET COCOA.

**3/4 CUP WATER**

**1 CUP SUGAR**

**1 VANILLA BEAN, SPLIT**

**3 1/4 CUPS OF ROASTED HAZELNUTS**

**21 OZ. OF DARK OR MILK CHOCOLATE**

**9 OZ. OF SEMI-SWEET COCOA**

*Chefs John Lehmann and Conny Züger holding a serving platter of
cocoa-covered, praline-filled Swiss Dreams*

## FRANCO-AMERICAN CHOCOLATIERS

### Guittard Chocolate Company
### *Burlingame, California*

Founded in 1868 on the San Francisco waterfront by Etienne Guittard, the Guittard Chocolate Company is a family affair. The firm has passed from father to son for generations. With this inheritance has come a true love for chocolate making. This love is translated into a personal attention to their products and a tradition of French methods.

Guittard has several product lines. The premium line is the E. Guittard Collection, named after founder Etienne. The E. Guittard Collection is based on the original handwritten recipes of Etienne, well before the days of chocolate mass production and over-sweetening. The collection includes both blends and single bean varietal chocolates. Guittard sources many of the single-bean varietals for the E. Guittard collection from plantations in Venezuela, Colombia and Equador. These plantations are familiar with the Guittard's heirloom methods, including bean fermentation and drying procedures. Later, the beans are French roasted, crushed into nibs and hulled, stone ground, refined into a thick paste, conched to give it a silky texture, and then tempered and molded. At each stage of the process the chocolate is constantly tasted, guaranteeing a high quality equaling that found in France.

In addition to the single-bean varietals, the E. Guittard collection includes bean blends. Guittard is lauded for its 64% *L'Harmonie* dark chocolate bars, characterized by light floral aromas and a clean, deep finish. Guittard also has a popular 38% milk chocolate known as *Soleil d'Or*.

## Other Chocolatiers to Know:

**Donnelly Chocolates**, *Santa Cruz, California*, hand-made by talented craftspersons

**Fran's Chocolates**, *Seattle, Washington*, presented in a jewelry box-like setting, Fran's masters American dark chocolate

**Recchiuti Confections**, *San Francisco, California*

**Ghirardelli**, *San Francisco, California*

**Lake Champlain Chocolates**, *Burlington, Vermont*, a favorite of many truffle lovers, these chocolates always provoke "oohs" and "aahs"

**Richart Design et Chocolat**, *New York, Tokyo*

**Vosges Haut-Chocolat**, *Chicago, Illinois*, lovely exotic truffles in varieties that include spices as well as nuts, a great chocolate investment

**XOX Truffles**, *San Francisco, California*

Left: Etienne Guittard

Below: Gary Guittard

Several North American chocolatiers have a French flair.
Clockwise from this Page: Posh Chocolat, Annea Shea Chocolates, Chocolot
Artisan Confections, Gateau et Ganache, William Dean Chocolates, L'Artisan
du Chocolat, DeansSweets, Oliver Kita Fine Confections

# UN RENDEZVOUS AVEC PLAISIR

# FRANCE GALL

Singer France Gall has been a French icon since her start on television in the mid-1960's. Though talented, popular, and with many albums, including work with French musical rogue Serge Gainsbourg, she was often known as "the wife of celebrity Michel Berger." In the 1980's the couple became very active in the humanitarian fight against famine in Africa. Eventually they bought a house in Dakar, Senegal, where France Gall would go during difficult times. In 1987 she released a hit album, called "Babacar," based on her African experiences.

*France Gall*

*Serge Gainsbourg*

Pour me faire apprendre la technique du piano, on me faisait miroiter une barre de chocolat en fin de leçon!

*To make me learn proper piano technique they would promise me a bar of chocolate at the end of the lesson!*

**- Michel Berger, French singer**

## Mon aéroplane
### France Gall

[*excerpt*]
Mon aéroplane...
Depuis ton départ est en panne...
Et pour toucher le ciel je n'ai plus, je n'ai plus
Que des nuages artificiels
Mon aéroplane...
Depuis ton départ est en panne...
Et pour toucher le ciel j'ai besoin, j'ai besoin
Que tu me prêtes tes ailes

Il y aura
Du thé de Chine et du réglisse
Et puis du chocolat
Tu verras
Nous irons plus au quai jadis
Mais viens vite chez moi
Je t'en supplie...

[*translation*]
My airplane...
Since you left has broken down...
and to touch the sky I no longer have,
I have only artificial clouds
My airplane...
Since you left has broken down...
And to touch the sky I need, I need
for you to lend me your wings

There will be
Tea from China and liquorice
And then some chocolate
You will see
We won't go anymore to yesterday's boarding gate
But come quickly to my home
I implore you...

*Chocolate flowers and chocolate bouquets,
from Le Fleuriste du Chocolat, Paris*

## LA FRANCOPHONIE CHOCOLATÉE

In today's world, English is the dominant language. It is the language of commerce, entertainment, science, and politics. But that position is not a monopoly, and French continues to be the second language of choice for a large number of people around the globe. Beyond the former colonies in America, the Caribbean, Africa, Polynesia and Indonesia, where French remains a lingua franca, French is still one of the most preferred languages for philosophy, diplomacy, and cuisine.

The French-speaking world (*la francophonie*) is a mosaic of colors and cultures, and this tapestry can be seen and heard in modern France. Music, fashion, and even food have all been enriched by the contribution of *la francophonie chocolatée*. Far from the days when Alexandre Dumas and Josephine Baker were the only well-known *gens de couleur*, now the French-speaking world enjoys scores of non-Gallic personalities and personages. Dishes like couscous, originally from North Africa, are a ubiquitous staple of many French households, and the love of the exotic continues to manifest itself profoundly within the French lifestyle.

*Alexandre Dumas, author of*
*"The Three Musketeers"*

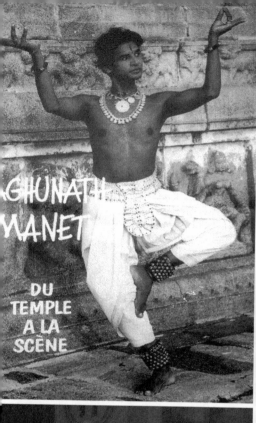

GHUNATH
MANET

DU
TEMPLE
A LA
SCÈNE

Et si on montait le son?

# COUSCOUS SUCRÉ WITH HONEY, RAISINS AND CACAO

This dish is for the 100% chocolate fanatic. If that is you, welcome to paradise. If you are a 35% fan, simply remove all chocolate from the recipe and sprinkle grated chocolate on the couscous at the end.

1. MELT CHOCOLATE.
2. PUT 1 CUP OF WATER IN SAUCE PAN, ADD RAISINS, COVER AND SIMMER FOR 10 MINUTES ON LOW HEAT.
3. ADD MILK, SALT, AND 1 TBS OF BUTTER. BRING TO SLOW BOIL.
4. STIR IN 1 TBS OF CHOCOLATE, REDUCE HEAT TO SIMMER FOR 1 MINUTE, THEN ADD COUSCOUS. STIR TO MAKE SURE THAT ALL THE COUSCOUS IS IN THE LIQUID. COVER AND REMOVE FROM HEAT. ALLOW TO SIT FOR SEVEN MINUTES.
5. ADD HONEY AND REMAINING BUTTER, COVER AND ALLOW TO SIT FOR THREE TO FOUR MINUTES SO THAT THE BUTTER AND HONEY WILL MELT AND DISSOLVE.
6. ADD CHOPPED ALMONDS AND 2 TBS OF CHOCOLATE, AND GENTLY STIR INTO COUSCOUS. FLUFF COUSCOUS WITH A FORK.

2/3 CUP MILK
1 CUP WATER
1/2 TSP SALT
1 CUP OF COUSCOUS (SEMOLINA)
5 TBS BUTTER, UNSALTED
1 TBS HONEY
3 OZ. SEMISWEET DARK CHOCOLATE, GRATED
1/3 CUP GOLDEN RAISINS
3 TBS OF CHOPPED ALMONDS, TOASTED OR BLANCHED (UNSALTED)
1 APPLE, CORED, PEELED, AND CHOPPED INTO SMALL CUBES (DICED)

## TO SERVE

PLACE COUSCOUS IN RAMEKIN. GARNISH WITH CHOPPED APPLE. SERVES 3 TO 4

# CREOLE HOT CHOCOLATE

The Caribbean islands of Martinique and Guadeloupe make up part of the French Antilles, and along with what is now Haiti were substantial symbols of French culture in the New World. The modern citizens of Martinique and Guadeloupe are still primarily French speaking, and they enjoy many of the bilateral benefits of a close relationship with the economic power of France. On Martinique it is very common for people to prepare a cup of hot chocolate in the morning, on special occasions, or perhaps with dessert. A favorite tradition is to have a mug of Creole hot chocolate with a nice piece of buttered bread. A simple combination, yet extremely savory, and worthy of promoting memories of days in the sun and on the beach.

1. MIX THE CORNSTARCH WITH THE WATER, STIR WELL TO MAKE SURE CORNSTARCH IS FULLY DISSOLVED. SET ASIDE.

2. IN A SAUCEPAN, ADD THE MILK, NUTMEG, CINNAMON STICKS, AND 1/4 TSP OF VANILLA. SLOWLY BRING TO A BOIL. STIR OCCASIONALLY.

3. ADD SUGAR AND STIR WELL TO DISSOLVE.

4. ADD THE CHOCOLATE TO THE MILK AND STIR SLOWLY FOR TWO MINUTES OVER MEDIUM-LOW HEAT TO ENSURE CHOCOLATE MELTS EVENLY.

5. ADD CORNSTARCH. LOWER HEAT TO SIMMER AND STIR REGULARLY FOR FIVE MINUTES, ALLOWING THE LIQUID TO THICKEN.

6. REMOVE CINNAMON STICKS, LET COOL SLIGHTLY AND SERVE. SERVES 4

4 CUPS OF MILK

2 CINNAMON STICKS

A PINCH OF NUTMEG

5 TBS OF GRANULATED SUGAR

1/2 TSP OF VANILLA EXTRACT

1 TBS OF CORNSTARCH

1 TBS OF COLD OR COOL WATER

4 TBS OF DARK CHOCOLATE, GRATED OR FINELY CHOPPED

# BANANA, STRAWBERRY & CHOCOLATE RIVIERA TART

**Stéphanie Ratineau, Côte d'Azur**, This recipe was originally contributed by Stéphanie Ratineau from the south of France, on the Côte d'Azur in the department of Var à la Seyne sur mer. Stéphanie has knowledge of a number of tropical chocolate dishes. She used 2 bananas and a slightly different ganache filling on this one, but to save you time we decided to use the version of ganache and pâte brisée already provided in this book. We have also added strawberries to the recipe, which adds to the tropical flavor, and renamed it "the Riviera."

1. USING A ROLLING PIN ON A FLAT SURFACE, ROLL THE PÂTE BRISÉE INTO A FLAT CIRCLE, LARGE AND THIN ENOUGH SO THAT IF FITS INTO A 9 OR 11 INCH TART PAN. PLACE IN PAN, MAKING SURE THAT THE DOUGH COATS THE BOTTOM AND SIDES OF THE PAN. USE THE ROLLING PIN TO TRIM EXCESS OF THE TART SHELL BY ROLLING ACROSS THE TOP EDGES OF THE TART PAN.

2. BLIND BAKE THE TART SHELL IN THE OVEN FOR 20 MINUTES AT 350ºF. TO BLIND BAKE, LINE THE TART SHELL WITH FOIL OR BAKING PARCHMENT PAPER, THEN FILL WITH DRIED BEANS, UNCOOKED RICE, OR BAKING STONES.

3. CUT BANANAS AND STRAWBERRIES INTO SLICES APPROXIMATELY 1/4 TO 1/3 INCH THICK.

4. REMOVE TART PAN FROM OVEN, REMOVE FOIL AND BAKING STONES FROM THE TOP OF THE TART SHELL.

5. LINE THE BOTTOM OF THE TART SHELL IN A CIRCULAR PATTERN WITH THE BANANA SLICES. SAVE 7-8 BANANAS SLICES FOR DECORATION.

6. POUR GANACHE FILLING OVER BANANAS IN TART PAN. PLACE DECORATIVE SLICES ON TOP OF GANACHE.

7. PLACE IN REFRIGERATOR TO CHILL FOR 3 HOURS.

**GANACHE (SEE FEATURED RECIPE)**

**PÂTE BRISÉE (SEE FEATURED RECIPE)**

**4 BANANAS**

**7 TO 15 STRAWBERRIES**

Author Monique Y. Wells is a good example of the longtime relationship that African-Americans and other people of color have had with the French and French culture. A native of Houston, Texas, Monique is a longtime resident of Paris. She left home at the age of 16 to attain the education that would allow her to pursue a career in veterinary pathology. After only six months of professional activity, Dr. Wells decided to pursue her dream to live and work in France. She moved to Paris in 1992. Inspired by her longing for foods from home, she explored the city's markets for ingredients with which she could recreate her favorite recipes. This, in addition to her involvement with a group called SISTERS, led her to write the award-winning cookbook, "*Food for the Soul: A Texas Expatriate Nurtures Her Culinary Roots in Paris.*" The book has been a great success, and was reviewed in Marie Claire Maison, Le Nouvel Economiste, La Lettre des Gourmands, the Washington Post, Publishers Weekly, CNN, Ebony, Essence, France Today, and the Los Angeles Times.

Her love of the city and her interest in African-American history in Paris also led her to co-author the book entitled "*Paris Reflections: Walks Through African-American Paris*," with Christiann Anderson.

*Since I moved to Paris, one of my most rewarding culinary experiences has been acquiring a taste for dark chocolate. To savor a morsel of 75% pure Madagascar or Java chocolate is simply heavenly. French chocolate has won my heart!*

**- Monique Y. Wells, author
"Food for the Soul:
A Texas Expatriate Nurtures
Her Culinary Roots in Paris"**

# CHOCOLATE QUAD

**Monique Y. Wells,**

This attractive, layered dessert is very RICH! It is widely enjoyed by my family and friends in Houston, and people in Paris love it too.

### FIRST LAYER

PREHEAT OVEN TO 350ºF. MIX TOGETHER THE FLOUR, BUTTER (OR MARGARINE), AND PECANS, AND PRESS INTO THE BOTTOM OF THE PAN TO MAKE A CRUST. BAKE 15 MINUTES AT 350ºF. REMOVE AND ALLOW TO COOL.

### SECOND LAYER

MIX CREAM CHEESE, POWDERED SUGAR, AND 1 CUP OF THE CRÈME FOUETTÉE OR "COOL WHIP". CAREFULLY SPREAD THIS ON TOP OF THE COOLED FIRST LAYER.

### THIRD & FOURTH LAYERS

1. STIR THE CHOCOLATE PUDDING MIX AND THE MILK TOGETHER IN A SEPARATE BOWL. SPREAD THIS CAREFULLY ONTO THE SECOND LAYER.

2. SPREAD THE REMAINDER OF THE CRÈME FOUETTÉE OR COOL WHIP* ONTO THE THIRD LAYER.

### TO SERVE

CUT INTO SQUARES OF THE DESIRED SIZE AND LIFT FROM THE PAN WITH A PIE SERVER OR SPATULA.

*AS A SUBSTITUTE FOR COOL WHIP, YOU CAN WHIP YOUR OWN CREAM OR USE CANNED CREME FOUETTÉE. AS WHIPPING CREAM BASICALLY DOUBLES ITS VOLUME WITH THE INCORPORATION OF AIR, START WITH SIX OUNCES OF IT. THE CANNED PRODUCT COMES IN 250 G CONTAINERS - ONE WILL SUFFICE, BUT IF YOU WISH TO BE LAVISH WITH YOUR FINAL LAYER, I'D ADVISE BUYING TWO. IF USING CANNED CREME FOUETTÉE, TOP THE DESSERT JUST BEFORE SERVING. OTHERWISE, THE WHIPPED TOPPING WILL DEFLATE.

1 CUP FLOUR

1/2 CUP BUTTER OR MARGARINE

1 CUP CHOPPED PECANS

8 OZ. CREAM CHEESE

1/2 - 1 CUP POWDERED SUGAR (OR TO TASTE)

12 OZ. CRÈME FOUETTÉE, OR 1 CONTAINER OF "COOL WHIP"*

3 (3.5 OZ) PACKAGES INSTANT CHOCOLATE PUDDING MIX

3 CUPS WHOLE MILK

PANS: 9 x 13-INCH BAKING PAN

## Chocolate Tokyo

This may be a surprise to many Westerners, but fine chocolate is big in Japan, and aside from the home grown brands, French-influenced chocolate is the biggest. From the packaging of individual bars, the decor and names of the boutiques, to the presentation of actual chocolate-coated desserts, the Japanese have an eye for detail and quality. Some of the greatest chocolatier and pastry names can be found in Tokyo alone, as well as others that are currently only great in Japan, including: Richart, La Maison du Chocolat, Décadence du Chocolat, Chocolat Bel Amer, Jean-Paul Hévin, Chocolatier Puissance, Theobroma - Musée du Chocolat, O2, Demel, Ecole Criollo, Pascal Café, Le Chocolat de H, Pierre Marcolini, Le Patissier Takagi, Patisserie Déffert, Masaki Nagashima, and Pierre Hermé Paris.

*Above: The Beach at Cap d'Ail, Côte d'Azur Below: Luxembourg Gardens, Paris*

## CHOCOLATE PROUST

Marcel Proust, that genius of French letters, grew up under the relentless yet loving scrutiny of a mother and grandmother for whom the journals of the Marquise de Sévigné were scripture. These ladies traveled with the Marquise's books and quoted her incessantly in their letters and conversation, including her thoughts on chocolate. In his own books, Proust writes long descriptions of food eaten in grand dining rooms and at home, the ingredients, and the talent and nature of the cook. Needless to say, chocolate shows up frequently. In fact, chocolate is mentioned several times during Proust's "In Search of Lost Time." The young narrator recalls "a work composed especially for ourselves... a cream of chocolate... laid before us, as light and fleeting as an occasional piece of music." Later, the topic that captures his attention most thoroughly is the chocolate cake they'll be having during tea:

> "On those tea party days... I felt that I could already behold
> the majesty of the chocolate cake... an architectural cake,
> as gracious and sociable as it was imposing, seemed to be
> enthroned there in case the fancy seized Gilberte to discrown
> it of its chocolate battlements and to hew down the steep,
> brown slopes of its ramparts... Better still, in proceeding
> in the demolition of this Babylonian pastry... she extracted
> for me from the crumbling monument a whole glazed slab
> jeweled with scarlet fruits in the Oriental style."

Proust continues to make references to chocolate in this remarkable work. For example, the superlative chocolate ices served at the Ritz hotel, or the chocolate soufflés that waiters raced to tables before they collapsed. Though the madeleine is the French sweet most often associated with Proust, the madeleine never receives from him such paragraphs of utter enthusiasm.

Proust's chocolate cakes epitomize the French way. In this view, chocolate is a splendid ingredient, to be put to subtle use, as in chocolate cream or soufflés, or worked to proportions of magnificence, as in a memorable chocolate cake.

*P Segal*
Chef and
Editor, "Proust Said That"

Below: The perfect music for creating or reading a book on chocolate, from Putumayo World Music. Above: Putumayo founders Dan Storper and Michael Kraus.

# Vocabulaire

## COMMON CHOCOLATE CUISINE INGREDIENTS

**Abricots**: apricots
**Agneau**: lamb
**Ail**: garlic
**Ananas**: pineapple
**Amande**: almond
**Banane**: banana
**Beurre**: butter
**Beurre de cacao**: cocoa butter
**Beurre non-salé**: unsalted butter
**Blancs d'oeufs**: egg whites
**Blé**: wheat
**Bouillon**: broth
**Cacao**: cocoa
**Cacao en fèves**: whole cocoa beans
**Canard**: duck
**Cannelle**: cinammon
**Carrottes**: carrots
**Cerise**: cherry
**Châtaigne**: chestnut
**Chocolat**: chocolate
**Chocolat au lait**: milk chocolate
**Chocolat belge**: belgium chocolate
**Chocolat blanc**: white chocolate, made of cocoa butter, sugar and milk
**Chocolat de couverture**: coating chocolate, chocolate coating
**Chocolat en poudre**: chocolate powder
**Chocolat instantané**: instant chocolate

**Chocolat noir**: dark chocolate
**Citron**: lemon
**Couscous**: couscous
**Crème**: cream
**Crème fraîche**: crème fraîche
**Crème fouettée**: whipped cream
**Dinde**: turkey
**Eau**: water
**Eau chaud**: warm water
**Eau froid**: cold water
**Eau tiède**: room temperature, lukewarm, tepid water
**Eclat de chocolat**: chocolate chip
**Estragon**: tarragon
**Extrait**: extract (as in, Vanilla extract)
**Farine**: flour
**Figues**: figs
**Fraises**: strawberries
**Framboises**: raspberries
**Fromage**: cheese
**Fruit confit**: crystallized, candied fruit
**Ganache**: a rich mixture of hot crème fraîche and chocolate, created by mixing the two and stirring until smooth. Can be used as a filling for bonbons or cakes, a glaze, as a base for truffles, and/or flavored or aromatised with fruits, coffee, tea, etc.
**Génoise**: French sponge cake
**Gianduja**: a filling, a paste consisting of milk chocolate and finely grated hazelnuts.

**Gingembre**: ginger

**Gingembre confit**: crystallized, candied ginger

**Glace**: ice, ice cream

**Gomme**: gum

**Jaunes d'oeufs**: egg yolks

**Lait**: milk

**Lapin**: rabbit

**Légume**: vegetable

**Levure (chimique)**: baking powder

**Macaron**: macaroon

**Marron**: chestnut

**Menthe**: mint

**Miel**: honey

**Miettes de chocolat**: chocolate crumbs

**Moutarde**: mustard

**Noisette**: hazelnut

**Noisette caramélisée**: caramelized hazelnut

**Noix de cajou**: cashew

**Noix de coco**: coconut

**Noix de macadam**: macadamia nuts

**Noix muscade**: nutmeg

**Nougat**: a filling which is made from honey and sugar, aerated with egg-white, and garnished with nuts or dried fruit

**Oeuf**: egg

**Orange**: orange

**Pain**: bread

**Pâte**: paste, dough

**Pâte à choux**: Cream puff paste (dough used in profiteroles, éclairs, cream puffs and beignets)

**Pâte à frire**: batter

**Pâte à glacer**: baker's chocolate

**Pâte à pain**: dough

**Pâte à tarte**: pastry

**Pâte brisée**: shortcrust pastry dough

**Pâte d'amandes** – almond paste, a filling made of almonds and sugar

**Pâte de cacao**: cocoa paste

**Pâte de chocolat noir**: dark chocolate paste

**Pêche**: peach

**Pectin**: ingredient used as a thickener, jelly-like in texture

**Pistache**: pistachio

**Poires**: pears

**Poivre**: pepper

**Poisson**: fish

**Pommes**: apples

**Pomme de terre**: potato

**Porc**: pork

**Potiron**: pumpkin

**Poudre de cacao**: cocoa powder

**Poudre de lait**: milk powder

**Poulet**: chicken

**Praline**: praline, made with hazelnuts and hot caramel, cooled, hardened, then crushed into a fine paste

**Prune**: plum

**Pruneau**: prune

**Pulpe de fruit**: fruit pulp

**Raisins**: grapes

**Raisins secs**: raisins

**Rhum**: rum

**Sel**: Salt

**Sirop de gingembre**: ginger syrup

**Soupe / potage**: soup

**Sucre**: sugar

**Sucre de canne**: cane sugar

**Tablette**: Bar of black chocolate

**Tablette de chocolat**: chocolate bar

**Truffes**: chocolate truffles

**Vanille**: vanilla

*Above: Traditional French chocolate molds. Molds courtesy of Carolyn Byrnes*

## Useful Descriptives

**froid**, froide: cold
**chaud,chaude**: hot
**bas, basse**: low
**sans**: without
**avec**: with
**puis, ensuite, après**: afterwards, thus

## Various Utensils

**ustensiles**: utensils
**casserole**: saucepan
**couteau**: knife
**cuillère**: spoon
**cuillère à cafe**: coffee spoon (approximately equivalent in measuring to a teaspoon)
**cuillère à soupe**: soup spoon (approximately equivalent in measuring to a tablespoon)
**fourchette**: fork
**marmite**: pot
**panier**: basket
**petite cuillère**: teaspoon
**poêle**: stove
**poêle a frire**: frying pan

## A Useful Expression

**à chacun son goût**: each to his/her own, everyone to his/her own taste

## USEFUL VERBS

**acheter**: to buy

**apporter**: to bring

**assaisonner**: to season

**battre**: to whisk, to beat

**boire**: to drink

**bouffer**: to eat

**bouillir**: to boil

**broyer**: to crush

**brûler**: to burn

**caraméliser**: to caramelize

**casser**: to break

**chauffer**: to heat, to warm

**commander**: to order

**comprendre**: to understand

**congéler**: to freeze

**coûter**: to cost

**couvrir**: to cover

**cuire**: to cook

**cuire à feu doux**: to cook over low heat or over a slow fire

**cuisiner**: to cook, to grill

**déguster**: to taste

**délayer**: to mix (with water, etc.)

**dîner**: to have dinner

**dorer**: to brown

**éplucher**: to peel

**étaler**: to spread

**éteindre [le four]:** to turn off, extinguish [the stove]

**flamber**: to flame

**fondre**: to melt, to dissolve

**frire**: to fry

**goûter**: to taste

**hacher**: to chop, mince

**manger**: to eat

**poivrer**: to add pepper as a seasoning

**préférer, aimer mieux**: to prefer

**prendre**: to take

**réchauffer**: to warm up, to reheat

**remuer**: to stir

**rendre**: to give back, return; to produce, make or render

**répondre**: to answer, to respond

**rôtir**: to roast

**saupoudrer**: to sprinkle (powdered sugar, for example)

**sauter**: to fry

**tartiner**: to spread, as in butter or chocolate

**vendre**: to sell

**verser**: to pour

**vouloir**: to want

# FRANÇAIS AU CHOCOLAT- ALPHABETICAL

## A

**acide citrique**: citric acid
**addition**: the restaurant check
**ajouter**: to add
**aliment**: food
**amidon**: starch
**amande**: almond
**amer**: bitter
**arôme**: aroma
**assiette**: plate
**assortiment**: selection, assortment

## B

**beignet**: fritter
**belge**: belgium
**beurre**: butter
**beurre de cacao**: cocoa butter
**boisson**: a drink
**boîte**: can, box
**bol**: traditional French cup shaped like a bowl
**bonbon**: sweets, candy, a delicacy
**bonbon de chocolat**: chocolate candy
**bouchées**: mouth-sized filled chocolate delicacies
**bouillon**: broth
**boulangerie**: bakery
**bouteille**: bottle

## C

**cabosse**: cocoa pod, fruit of the cocoa tree, containing seeds which are extracted and treated and processed to produce chocolate
**cacao**: cocoa
**cacao en fèves**: whole cocoa beans
**cacaoyer**: cocoa tree, originating from south america

**carafe**: carafe
**carte**: menu, card
**cassure**: break
**chardons**: thistles
**chocolat**: chocolate
**chocolat au lait**: milk chocolate
**chocolat belge**: belgium chocolate
**chocolat blanc**: white chocolate, made of cocoa butter, sugar and milk
**chocolat chaud**: hot chocolate
**chocolat de couverture**: coating chocolate, chocolate coating
**chocolat en poudre**: chocolate powder
**chocolat instantané**: instant chocolate
**chocolat noir**: dark chocolate
**chocolatier**: chocolate maker
**comestibles**: food
**commerçant(e)**: shopkeeper
**confiserie de chocolat**: chocolate confectionery
**congélateur**: freezer
**coq**: rooster (*coq au vin*: chicken cooked in wine)
**croquant**: crisp, crunchy
**croûte**: crust
**cru**: raw
**cuillère à cafe**: coffee spoon (approximately equivalent in measuring to a teaspoon)
**cuillère à soupe**: soup spoon (approximately equivalent in measuring to a tablespoon)
**cuisine**: food, cooking, kitchen
**cuisinière**: stove, the cook (female)

## D

**déjeuner**: lunch

**dessert**: dessert
**dinde**: turkey
**le dîner**: dinner
**dragée**: sugared almond

**E**
**eclat de chocolat**: chocolate chip
**enrobage**: coating
**entrée**: first course
**épicerie**: grocery store
**extrait**: extract

**F**
**fabricant de chocolat**: chocolate manufacturer
**farci**: stuffed
**fève**: bean, seed
**fèves de cacao brutes**: raw cocoa beans
**fèves de cacao torréfiées**: roasted cocoa beans
**flambé**: flamed with brandy, rum, etc
**fourré**: filled
**frais (fraîche)**: fresh
**friandises**: sweets
**frigo**: the fridge
**fruit confit**: crystallized, candied fruit
**fumé**: smoked

**G**
**ganache**: a rich mixture of crème fraîche and chocolate, created by mixing the two and stirring until smooth. can be used as a filling for bonbons or cakes, a glaze, as a base, and/or flavored or aromatised with fruits, coffee, tea, etc.
**gianduja**: a filling, a paste consisting of milk chocolate and finely grated hazelnuts.

**gingembre confit**: crystallized, candied ginger
**gomme**: gum
**goût**: the taste
**le goûter**: afternoon snack

**H**
**heure**: hour
**hors-d'oeuvre**: appetizers

**M**
**magasin**: store, shop
**marbre**: marble
**marbré**: marbled, mottled
**marché**: marketplace, market
**marron**: chestnut
**menthe**: mint
**mets**: a dish (food)
**miel**: honey
**miettes de chocolat**: chocolate crumbs
**mixer**: blender
**la mode**: fashion
**le mode**: form; way of life
**moule**: mold

**N**
**napolitain**: a small square shaped piece of chocolate
**nibs**: the fleshy part of the interior of the cocoa bean.
**noisette**: hazelnut
**noisette caramélisée**: caramelized hazelnut
**non fourrés**: non filled
**nougat**: a filling which is made from honey and sugar, aerated with egg-white, and garnished with nuts or dried fruit
**nourriture**: food

**P**

**palets**: disks

**pâte**: paste

**pâte à frire**: batter

**pâte à pain**: dough

**pâte à tarte**: pastry

**pâte brisée**: shortcrust pastry

**pâte d'amandes**: almond paste, a filling made of almonds and sugar

**pâte de cacao**: cocoa paste

**pâte de chocolat noir**: dark chocolate paste

**pâtisserie**: pastry shop, pastry

**pectin**: ingredient used as a thickener, jelly-like in texture

**petit carré chocolat**: small chocolate squares

**petit déjeuner**: breakfast

**pistache**: pistachio

**placard**: the cupboard

**plat**: dish (plat du jour), course

**poudre de cacao**: cocoa powder

**poudre de lait**: milk powder

**pourboire**: the tip

**prix**: price

**pulpe de fruit**: fruit pulp

**R**

**raisins**: grapes

**raisins secs**: raisins

**réfrigérateur**: the refrigerator

**repas**: meal

**rhum**: rum

**rôti**: roast

**S**

**saveur du cacao**: flavor of the cocoa

**savoureux**: tasty

**service compris**: tip included

**sommelier**: the wine steward

**sirop de gingembre**: ginger syrup

**succulent**: succulent

**sucre**: sugar

**sucre de canne**: cane sugar

**suisse**: Swiss

**T**

**tablette**: bar of chocolate

**tablette de chocolat**: chocolate bar

**tasse**: cup

**temps**: time

**tranche**: a slice

**truffes**: chocolate truffles

**U**

**ustensiles**: utensils

**V**

**vanille**: vanilla

**velouté**: velvety

**vite**: quickly

**volaille**: poultry

# Recipe Contributors

**Absinthe Brasserie**
398 Hayes Street
San Francisco, California
Tél: 415.551.1590
www.absinthe.com
pp. 67

**Bouchon**
6534 Washington St.
Yountville, California 94599
Tél: 707.944.8037
www.bouchonbistro.com
pp. 60

**Broussard's Restaurant**
819 Conti
New Orleans, Louisiana 70112
Tél: 504.581.3866
www.broussards.com
pp. 117-118

**Bistrot Bruno Loubet**
St John's Square,
86-88 Clerkenwell Road, London
Tél: 44 (0)20 7324 4455
www.bistrotbrunoloubet.com
pp. 34

**Cafe Andree**
Hotel Rex
562 Sutter Street
San Francisco, California 94102
Tél: 800.433.4434
www.jdvhospitality.com
pp. 69

**Cafe de la Presse**
352 Grant Avenue
San Francisco, California
Tél: 415.249.0900
www.cafedelapresse.com
pp. 38

**Cafe Matou**
1846 N. Milwaukee Ave
Chicago, Illinois 60647
Tél: 773.384.8911
www.cafematou.com
pp. 102

**Carlos'**
429 Temple
Highland Park, Illinois 60035
Tél: 847.432.0770
www.carlos-restaurant.com
pp. 101

**Chef Isabelle Alexandre**
pp. 41

**Le Cordon Bleu**
8, rue Leon Delhomme
Paris
France
Tél: 01 53.68.22.50
www.cordonbleu.edu
pp. 36, 129

**French Pastry School**
226 W Jackson Blvd, Suite 106
Chicago, Illinois 60606
Tél: 312.726.2419
www.frenchpastryschool.com
pp. 32, 105

**John Lehmann**
CP 54
CH-1644 Avry-dt-Pont
Switzerland
Tél: 41 26.915.09.50
www.patisserie.ch
www.LePAIN.ch
pp. 150

## Jean-Paul Hévin
23 bis, avenue de la Motte-Picquet
Paris
Tél: 01 45.51.77.48
www.jphevin.com

## Left Bank
507 Magnolia Avenue
Larkspur, California
Tél: 415.927.3331
www.leftbank.com

## Louisiana School of Cooking & Cajun Store
Lafayette, Louisiana
Tél: 337.983.0896
www.louisianaschoolofcooking.com

## La Note, Restaurant Provençal
2377 Shattuck Avenue
Berkeley, California 94704
Tél: 510.843.1535
www.lanoterestaurant.com

## Olde Victorian Inn
914 North Ramport Street
New Orleans, Louisiana 70116
Tél: 800.725.2446 (toll free)

## Patisserie Kubler
29 avenue des Vosges
Strasbourg
France
Tél:  03 88.35.22.27
www.kubler.fr

## Promenades Gourmandes
187, rue du Temple
Paris
France
Tél: 01 48.04.56.84
www.promenadesgourmandes.com

## Restaurant Jean-Louis
61 Lewis Street
Greenwich, Connecticut 06830
Tél: 203.622.8450
www.restaurantjeanlouis.com

## Restaurant Lulu
816 Folsom Street
San Francisco, California 94107
Tél: 415.495.5775
www.restaurantlulu.com

## Valencia Chocolates
New York
valenciachocolates@hotmail.com

## Le Zinc
4063 24th Street
San Francisco, California
Tél: 415.647.9400
www.lezinc.com

## Zoe Bistro
W New Orleans
333 Poydras Street
New Orleans, Louisiana 70130
Tél: 504.525.9444
www.whotels.com

**Gerri Chanel**
Alliance Française
Hartford, Connecticut

**Monique Y. Wells**
Author, "Food For The Soul: A Texas
    Expatriate Nurtures Her Culinary
    Roots In Paris"
www.parisfoodforthesoul.com

**Stéphanie Ratineau**
Côte d'Azur
France

also:

**Suzanne C. Toczyski, Ph.D**.
Chair, Dept. of Modern Languages &
    Literatures
Sonoma State University
(pictured, left)

## Recipe Contributions: Individuals

**André K. Crump**
TCB-Cafe Publishing
San Francisco, California

**Anne De Kouchkovsky**
Lycée Français la Pérouse
The International French School
San Francisco, California
www.lelycee.org

**Caroline Isautier-Rougeot**
Editor / Editrice
Frenchparents.net
**Danielle Avidan**
Alliance Française
Pacific Palisades/Los Angeles
California

## Le Colonel Chabert (excerpts in French)
## by Honoré de Balzac

Un coup frappé à la porte de l'étude interrompit la phrase de la prolixe requête. Cinq clercs bien endentés, aux yeux vifs et railleurs, aux têtes crépues, levèrent le nez vers la porte, après avoir tous crié d'une voix de chantre : "Entrez." Boucard resta la face ensevelie dans un monceau d'actes, nommés - broutille - en style de Palais, et continua de dresser le mémoire de frais auquel il travaillait.

L'étude était une grande pièce ornée du poêle classique qui garnit tous les antres de la chicane. Les tuyaux traversaient diagonalement la chambre et rejoignaient une cheminée condamnée sur le marbre de laquelle se voyaient divers morceaux de pain, des triangles de fromage de Brie, des côtelettes de porc frais, des verres, des bouteilles, et la tasse de chocolat du Maître clerc.

L'odeur de ces comestibles s'amalgamait si bien avec la puanteur du poêle chauffé sans mesure avec le parfum particulier aux bureaux et aux paperasses, que la puanteur d'un renard n'y aurait pas été sensible.

...

"Monsieur, répondit-il, j'ai déjà eu l'honneur de vous prévenir que je ne pouvais expliquer mon affaire qu'à M. Derville, je vais attendre son lever. "

Boucard avait fini son addition. Il sentit l'odeur de son chocolat, quitta son fauteuil de canne, vint à la cheminée, toisa le vieil homme, regarda le carrick et fit une grimace indescriptible. Il pensa probablement que, de quelque manière que l'on tordît ce client, il serait impossible d'en extraire un centime ; il intervint alors par une parole brève, dans l'intention de débarrasser l'étude d'une mauvaise pratique.

" Ils vous disent la vérité, monsieur. Le patron ne travaille que pendant la nuit. Si votre affaire est grave, je vous conseille de revenir à une heure du matin."

Le plaideur regarda le Maître clerc d'un air stupide, et demeura pendant un moment immobile. Habitués à tous les changements de physionomie et aux singuliers caprices produits par l'indécision ou par la rêverie qui caractérisent les gens processifs, les clercs continuèrent à manger, en faisant autant de bruit avec leurs mâchoires que doivent en faire des chevaux au râtelier, et ne s'inquiétèrent plus du vieillard.

# RESOURCES

*Enrobing*

## Retail · Boutiques · Chocolatiers · Patisseries

### United States

Bittersweet, the Chocolate Cafe
5427 College Avenue
Oakland, CA 94618
Tél: 510-654-7159
www.bittersweetcafe.com

Cocoa Bella Chocolates
2102 Union Street
San Francisco, CA 94123
Tél: 415-931-6213
www.cocoabellachocolates.com

The Chocolate Truffle
31 St. James Avenue
Boston, MA 02116
Tél: 617.423.9400
www.thechocolatetruffle.com

The Chocolate Truffle
204 West Cummings Park
Woburn, MA 01801
Tél: 781.933.4616

Fauchon
442 Park Avenue
New York, New York 10022
Tél: 212.308.5919
www.fauchon

Fran's Chocolates
2594 NE University Village
Seattle, WA 98105
Tél: 206.528.9969

Ghirardelli
900 North Point Street
San Francisco, CA 94109
Tél: 415.771.4903
www.Ghirardelli.com

Ghirardelli
Soda Fountain & Chocolate Shop
801 Lincoln Rd
Miami Beach, FL 33139
Tél: 305.532.2538

Jacques Torres Chocolate
66 Water Street
Brooklyn, New York 11201
Tél: 718.875.9772
www.mrchocolate.com

Lake Champlain Chocolates
2653 Waterbury-Stowe Road
Waterbury Center, VT 05677
Tél: 802.241.4150
www.lakechamplainchocolates.com

La Maison du Chocolat
1018 Madison Avenue
New York, New York
Tel : 212.744.7117
www.lamaisonduchocolat.com

Scharffen Berger Chocolate Maker
Ferry Building Marketplace
One Ferry Building
San Francisco, California 94111
Tél: 415.905.5300
www.scharffenberger.com

Vosges Haut-Chocolat
520 N. Michigan Avenue
Chicago, Illinois 60611
Tél: 888.301.yumm (9866)

Vosges Haut-Chocolat
132 Spring Street
New York, New York 10012
Tél: 212.625.2929
www.VosgesChocolate.com

XOX Truffles
754 Columbus Avenue
San Francisco, California 94133
Tél: 415.421.4814
www.xoxtruffles.com

### Australia

Sweet William Chocolates
4 William Street
Paddington
Sydney, NSW 2021
Tél: 61 (0)2.9331.5468

### Canada

Chocolate Arts
2037 West 4th Avenue
Vancouver BC Canada V6J 1N3
Tél: 877.739.0475
www.chocolatearts.com

Chocolaterie Bernard Callebaut
Signal Hill Centre
5771 Signal Hill Centre SW
Calgary, AB T3H 3P8
Tél: 403.217.1700
www.bernardcallebaut.com

Les Chocolats Martine Inc.
5 rue Ste-Anne
Ville-Marie
Quebec
Tél: 819.622.0146
www.chocolatmartine.com

### France

A L'Etoile d'Or
30, rue Fontaine
Paris
Tél: 01 48.74.59.55

A la Petite Fabrique
12, rue Saint-Sabin
Paris
Tél: 01 48.05.82.02

A la Reine Astrid
16, rue du Cherche Midi
Paris
Tél: 01 42.84.07.02
Paris

A la Reine Astrid
33, rue de Washington
Paris
Tél : 01 45.63.60.39

Ariane, Espace Chocolat
30, rue Legendre
Paris
Tél: 01 47.63.52.94

Bernachon
42, Cours Franklin Roosevelt
Lyon
Tél: 04 78.24.37.98

Chocolaterie Beline
5, place St Nicolas
Le Mans
Tél : 02 43.28.00.43

Christian Constant
37, rue d'Assas
Paris
Tél: 01 53.63.15.15

Christian Saunal
31 Avenue des Minimes
Toulouse

Dalloyou
99-101, rue de Faubourg Saint-Honoré
Paris
Tél: 01 43.59.18.10
www.Dalloyou.fr

Debauve & Gallais
30, rue des Saints-Pères
Paris
Tél: 01 45.48.54.67
www.debauve-et-gallais.com

Debauve & Gallais
33, rue Vivienne
Paris
Tél: 01 40.39.05.50
www.debauve-et-gallais.com

Deleans
20 Rue Ceres
Reims

De Neuville
14, rue des Petits Carreaux
Paris
Tél: 01 40.26.30.50
www.deneuville.fr

De Neuville
27, rue de Bretagne
Paris
Tél: 01 42.72.20.91

Fauchon
26, place de la Madeleine
Paris
Tél: 01 47.42.60.11
www.fauchon.com

La Fontaine au Chocolat(Michel Cluizel)
201, rue Saint-Honoré
Paris
Tél: 01 42.44.11.66
www.fontaineauchocolate.com

Fouquet
22, rue François 1er
Paris
Tél: 01 47.23.30.36

Hédiard
21, place de la Madeleine
Paris
Tél: 01 42.66.44.36
www.hediard.fr

Jadis et Gourmande
88, boulevard de Port-Royal
Paris
Tél: 01 40.47.64.64

Jean-Paul Hévin
3, rue Vavin
Paris
Tél: 01 43.54.09.85
www.jphevin.com

Jean-Paul Hévin
23 bis, avenue de la Motte-Picquet
Paris
Tél: 01 45.51.77.48

Joel Durand
5 Quai Chateaubriand
Rennes

Ladurée
16, rue Royale
Paris
Tél: 01 42.60.21.79
www.laduree.fr

La Maison du Chocolat
225, rue du Faubourg Saint-Honoré
Paris
Tél: 01 42.27.39.44
www.lamaisonduchocolat.com

La Maison du Chocolat
52, rue François 1er
Paris
Tél: 01 47.23.38.25

La Maison du Chocolat
89, rue Raymond Poincaré
Paris
Tél: 01 40.67.77.88

Lenôtre
44, rue d'Auteuil
Paris
Tél: 01 45.24.52.52

Marquise de Sévigné
32, place de la Madeleine
Paris
Tél: 01 42.65.19.47
www.marquise-de-sevigne.com

Michel Chaudun
149, rue de l'Université,
Paris
Tél: 01 47.53.74.40

Palomas
2, rue Colonel Chambonnet
Lyon
Tél: 04 78.37.74.60

Patisserie Kubler
29 avenue des Vosges
Strasbourg
Tél: 03 88.35.22.27
www.kubler.fr

Pierre Hermé, Patissier
72, rue Bonaparte
Paris
Tél: 01 43.54.47.77

Richart
258, boulevard Saint-Germain
Paris
Tél: 01 45.55.66.00

Seve Chocolates
62, avenue Lanessan
Champagne au Mont d'Or
Tél : 04 78.35.04.21
www.chocolat-seve.com

Thierry Mulhaupt - Patisserie
18, rue du Vieux Marché aux Poissons
Strasbourg
Tel : 03 88.23.15.02

Zugmeyer
4 Boulevard Agutte Sembat
Grenoble
Tél: 04 76.46.32.40
www.zugmeyer.fr

## Belgium

Chocolat Manon
9-A Chaussee de Louvain
Brussels
Tél: 02 217.64.09

Corne Toison D'Or
53 rue Marche aux Poulet
Brussels
Tél: 02 512.23.60

Galler
Grand Place
Brussels
Tél: 02 502.02.66

Godiva
Grand Place 22
Brussels
Tél: 02 511.25.37

Les Jardins du Chocolat
Place de Lille 10
Tournai
Tél: 06 984.78.16

Leonidas
Rue au Beurre 34
Brussels
Tél: 02 512.87.37

La Maison du Chocolat
67 rue Marche-aux-Herbes
Brussels
Tél: 02 513.78.92

Marcolini
Place du Grand Sablon 39
Brussels
Tél: 02 514.12.06

Mary Chocolatier
Rue Royale 37
Brussels
Tél: 02 217.45.00

Neuhaus
Gallerie de la Reine
Brussels
Tél: 02 512.63.59

Wittamer
Place du Grand Sablon 12
Brussels
Tél: 02 512.37.42

## Switzerland

Blondel
5, rue de Bourg
Lausanne
Tél: 41 21 323.44.74

La confiserie Schober
Napfgasse 4
Zurich
Tél: 41 1 251.80.60

Sprungli confiserie
Paradeplatz - Bahnhofstrasse 21
Zurich
Tél: 41 1 224.47.11

## Japan

Jean-Paul Hévin
Isetan Shinjuku
Shinjuku 3-chome
Shinjuku-ku Tokyo 160-0022
Tél : 81 (0)3 3351.7882

Jean-Paul Hévin
Andersen Hiroshima 7-1 Hondori
Naka-ku Hiroshima 730-0035
Tél : 81 (0)8 2247.2403

Madame Setsuko Tokyo-Japon
7-1-14, Ohmori-Nishi
Ohta-Ku – 143-85 Tokyo
Tél : 81 (0)3 3763.5115

## Cafe & Restaurant

Angelina's
226, rue de Rivoli
Paris
France
Tél: 01 47.27.88.56

Carette
4, Place du Trocadéro
Paris
France

Fauchon
26-28-30 Place de la Madeleine
Paris
France
Tél: 01 47.42.60.11

Fauchon
442 Park Avenue
New York, New York 10022
USA
Tél: 212.308.5919
www.fauchon

Il Palazzo
Hotel Normandy
7, rue de l'Echelle
Paris
France
Tél: 01 42.60.91.20

Jean-Paul Hévin
Salon de thé & chocolat
231, rue Saint-Honore
Paris
France
Tél: 01 55.35.35.96
www.jphevin.com

Ladurée
75, avenue Champs-Elysées
Paris
France
Tél: 01 40.75.08.75
www.laduree.fr

Ladurée
16, rue Royale
Paris
France
Tél: 01 42.60.21.79

La Maison du Chocolat
1018 Madison Avenue
New York, NY
USA
Tel: 212.744.7117
www.lamaisonduchocolat.com

World Bar
Printemps-Homme
5th floor
Paris
France

## Tours

Asher's Chocolates
80 Wambold Road
Souderton, PA  18964
USA
Tél: 215.721.3276
www.ashers.com

Le Chocolatier Manon
Rue Tilmont 64
Brussels
Belgium
Tel: 02 425.2632

Ecole Chocolat
France
www.ecocoa.net

La Fonderie
Rue Ransfort 27
Brussels
Belgium
Tél: 02 410.99.50

Lake Champlain Chocolates
750 Pine Street
Burlington VT 05401
USA
Tél: 800.465.5909
www.lakechamplainchocolates.com

Promenade Gourmandes
Paule Caillat
187, rue du Temple
Paris
France
Tél: 01 48.04.56.84
www.promenadesgourmandes.com

Scharffen Berger Chocolate Maker
914 Heinz Avenue
Berkeley, California  94710
USA
Tél: 510.981.4066
www.scharffenberger.com

TCHO Chocolate,
17 Pier,
San Francisco, CA
USA
Tél: 415.981.0189
www.tcho.com

Valrhona
14 avenue du Président Roosevelt
B.P. 40
Tain L'Hermitage Cedex
France
www.valrhona.com

## Classes & Instruction

Academie Culinaire de Montreal
360, Champ-de-Mars
Montreal, Qc., H2Y 3Z3
Canada
Tél: 514.393.8111
www.academieculinaire.com

Alliance Française
www.alliancefr.org (worldwide)
www.afusa.org (USA)

The Chocolate Society
www.chocolate.co.uk
United Kingdom

Le Cordon Bleu
8, rue Leon Delhomme
75015 Paris
France
Tél: 01 53.68.22.50
www.cordonbleu.edu

Le Cordon Bleu Corporate Office
40 Enterprise Avenue
Secaucus, NJ 07094-2517
USA
Telephone: 201 617 5221
www.cordonbleu.edu

Ecole Chocolat
USA / France / Canada
www.ecocoa.net

Ecole du Grand Chocolat
Quai Général de Gaulle
Tain L'hermitage
France

French Pastry School
226 W Jackson Blvd, Suite 106
Chicago, Illinois 60606
USA
Tél: 312.726.2419
www.frenchpastryschool.com

Louisiana School of Cooking & Cajun Store
Chef Patrick Mould
Lafayette, Louisiana
USA
Tél: 337.983.0896
www.louisianaschoolofcooking.com

Promenade Gourmandes
Paule Caillat
187, rue du Temple
Paris
France
Tél: 01 48.04.56.84
www.promenadesgourmandes.com

Université du Chocolat
Institut d'Études Supérieures des Arts
5, avenue de l'Opéra
Paris
France
Tél: 01 42.86.57.01
www.iesa.fr

## Associations

Alliance Française
www.alliancefr.org (worldwide)
www.afusa.org (USA)

The Chocolate Society
United Kingdom
www.chocolate.co.uk

Club des Croqueurs de Chocolat
France
www.croqueurschocolat.com

Club du Chocolat aux Palais
62, rue de Rennes
Paris
France
Tél:06 87.27.40.60

Confederation Nationale des Chocolatiers
Confiseurs de France
103 rue Lafayette
Paris
France
Tél: 01 42.85.18.20
www.chocolatiers.fr

L'Académie Française du Chocolat et de la
Confiserie
103 rue Lafayette
Paris
France

La Confrerie des Chocolatiers de France
103 rue Lafayette
Paris
France

Corporation des Pâtissiers, Confiseurs,
Chocolatiers et Glaciers du Bas-Rhin
15, rue du Parc Oberhausbergen
Strasbourg Cedex
France
Tél: 03 88.56.16.16
http://patissiers.webcd.fr

Association des Relais Desserts
Confédération de la Pâtisserie
31 rue Marius Alfan
Levallois Perret Cedex
France

Association "Les Relais du Chocolat"
5 place de la République
Valence
France
Tél : 04 75.43.05.28

Tradition Gourmande
20 boulevard Victor Hugo
Nîmes
France
Tél : 04 66.67.35.12

Association "KFE-KKO"
34, avenue des Champs Elysées
Paris
France
Tél/Fax: 01 60.05.80.01

Confédération Nationale de la Pâtisserie
Confiserie Chocolaterie Glacerie de France
31, rue Marius Aufan
Levallois Perret Cedex
France
Tél : 01 40.89.96.70

Fédération des Pâtissiers Traiteurs Glaciers
Confiseurs de Paris-Île de France
31, rue Marius Aufan
Levallois Perret Cedex
Tél.: 01 40.89.92.95
www.federationpatissiers.fr.st

Confédération Nationale des Desserts et des
Douceurs
64, Rue de Caumartin
Paris
France
Tél : 01 48.74.72.28

World Cocoa Foundation
8320 Old Courthouse Road
Suite 300
Vienna, VA 22182
USA
Tél: 703.790.5011
www.chocolateandcocoa.org

## Museums

Le Chocolatrium
Michel Cluizel
Avenue de Conches
Damville
France
Tel: 02 32.35.20.75

Musee de la Patisserie
Chateau de Harze, Route de Bastogne
Harze (Aywaille)
Belgium
Tél: 328 621.20.33

Museum of Cocoa and Chocolate
13 Grand-Place
Brussels
Belgium
Tél: 320 514.20.48
www.mucc.be

Museum Temple of Chocolate Cote D'Or
Brusselsesteenweg 450
Halle
Belgium
Tél: 02 362.37.47

Choco-Musée Érico
634, rue Saint-Jean Faubourg
Saint-Jean Baptiste Québec
QC Canada G1R 1P8
Canada
Tél: 418.524.2122
www.chocomusee.com

Le Musée du chocolat
14 avenue Beau Rivage
Biarritz
France
Tél: 05 59.24.50.50

# BIBLIOGRAPHY

**For Chocolate History, by Dr. Suzanne Toczyski**

Foster, Nelson & Linda S. Cordell. *Chilies to Chocolate: Food the Americas Gave the World.* Tucson: U of Arizona Press, 1992.

Furetiére, Antoine. *Dictionnaire universel.* 3 vols. La Haye and Rotterdam, 1690.

Hoffmann, Kathryn A. *Society of Pleasures: Interdisciplinary Readings in Pleasure and Power during the Reign of Louis XIV.* New York: St. Martin's Press, 1997.

Lang, Jenifer Harvey. Larousse gastronomique: The New American Edition of the World's Greatest Culinary Encyclopedia. New York: Crown Publishers, Inc., 1984.

Lekatsas, Barbara. "Inside the Pastilles of the Marquis de Sade," in Szogyi 99-107.

Seaman, David W. "Chocolate Imagery in Avant-Garde Art," in Szogyi 93-98.

Sévigné, Marie de Rabutin-Chantal, Marquise de. *Correspondance.* Ed. Roger Duchêne. 3 vols. Paris: Gallimard, 1972.

Szogyi, Alex. *Chocolate: Food of the Gods.* Westport, CT: Greenwood Press, 1997.

Tzara, Tristan. *Oeuvres completes.* Vol. I. Paris, Flammarion, 1975-1977.

White, Erdmute Wenzel. "Chocolate for Prose: Marcel Duchampís *Chocolate Grinder* and *The Large Glass*," in Szogyi 67-84.

Young, Allen M. *The Chocolate Tree: A Natural History of Cacao.* Washington & London: Smithsonian Institution Press, 1994.

**Other Recommended**

Terrio, Susan J., *Crafting the Culture and History of French Chocolate,* University of California Press, 2001

# REVIEWS OF "CHOCOLATE FRENCH"
## 1st & 2nd EDITIONS

*Perfect for every chocoholic Francophile alive!*

**- France Today magazine**

*CHOCOLATE FRENCH is an elegant and highly recommended addition to the cookbook collections of dedicated chocolate lovers everywhere!*

**- Midwest Book Review**

*A TREAT FOR ANYONE WHO SAVORS the allure of chocolate and of the French lifestyle.*

**- Wine Country Living Magazine**

*Little-known details about chocolate and those who consume it are packed into the pages of CHOCOLATE FRENCH.*

**- Oakland Tribune**

*AS A FRANCOPHILE AND A CHOCOHOLIC, this book, with its mix of chocolate history, recipes and passages about chocolate in French, gratified both of my addictions.*

**- Frenchfood.About.com**

*AND for a Francophile or chocolate lover, pick up a copy of 'CHOCOLATE FRENCH: Recipes, Language, and Directions to Francaise au Chocolat'*

**- Seattle Times**

Made in the USA
Lexington, KY
23 November 2011